How to Talk
to Your
Husband

Library of Congress Cataloging-in-Publication Data

McDermott, Patti.
     [How to talk to your husband]
     How to talk to your husband : How to talk to your wife / Patti
McDermott.
          p.   cm.
     Two books back to back.
     Includes bibliographical references.
     ISBN 0-8092-3682-6 (pbk.)
     1. Communication in marriage.   2. Interpersonal
communication.   3. Marriage.   I. McDermott, Patti. How to
talk to your wife.   II. Title.   III. Title: How to talk to your
wife.   IV. Title: How to talk to your husband : How to talk to
your wife.
HQ734.M4424   1994
646.7'8—dc20
                                                                94-20943
                                                                CIP

Published by Contemporary Books, Inc.
Two Prudential Plaza, Chicago, Illinois 60601-6790
Manufactured in the United States of America
International Standard Book Number: 0-8092-3682-6
10   9   8   7   6   5   4   3   2   1

For my husband, George Boroczi.
Still talking—and listening—after all these years.

Contents

Acknowledgments

I want to thank all my clients, past and present, for sharing their relationship issues with me.

I also want to thank my agents, Betsy Amster and Angela Miller, for their belief in me. As well as being my agent, Betsy has been—at various times—my editor, handholder, and cheerleader. She's a terrific friend. Betsy's initial encouragement is also what prompted me to write this book.

I'm grateful to my editor at Contemporary, Gene Brissie, for trusting in my vision of this book and giving me free rein to develop my ideas. I'd also like to thank Elena Anton Delaney for doing such a fine job of copyediting the manuscript.

My sister, Joanne Fahnestock, enthusiastically supported me throughout the writing of this book, as she has with everything in my life. Susan Cox shared some interesting ideas about relationships. Annette DiSano listened and made suggestions during our long walks with the kids. Beverly Engel provided useful feedback after reading parts of the book. During our monthly breakfasts, Alan Fox heard my progress reports about the book and offered his own thoughts and encouragement along the way.

Also, thanks to Kenna Crabtree for patiently answering my endless computer questions.

Finally, I wish to express my appreciation and love for my husband, George Boroczi, to whom this book is dedicated, and for my kids, Scott, Kim, Dylan, and Kyle. I am fortunate indeed to have such a remarkable family.

Introduction

Some of my most important work as a couples therapist comes from acting as an interpreter. No matter what issue brings a couple to therapy—arguments about sex, intimacy, kids, money—communication is usually at the heart of the problem.

Even though you and your husband use the same words, it may often seem as if you're speaking a different language. Ask your husband for the definition of the term *shared housework*, and you will see what I mean. Ditto for the term *leisure activity*. I'd wager that to your husband leisure activity means watching TV or playing sports. To you the term probably means doing activities with your family, reading a book, or doing housework.

Even if you and your husband are the most liberated couple on the planet, chances are you each speak a different language. That's because our society still pegs people by gender, and in our culture men and women learn different ways of communicating. In general, women often talk to get close and to feel connected, whereas men frequently talk to assert opinions or to give information. Most men still don't divulge their feelings or thoughts to the extent that women do.

For instance, when your husband says "I want to be alone," he usually means just that, and he doesn't take kindly to being pursued by you with questions like "What's wrong? Are you angry? Will you talk to me?" If you say "I want to be alone," you might mean "Pursue me" because you're feeling hurt or left out. Your husband doesn't get the hint, however, because he thinks you mean what *he* means when he says "I want to be alone." So he says "okay" and goes back to watching TV. (A good rule of thumb: don't give your husband subtle hints—he won't get them, or if he does he's likely to ignore them.)

In therapy, spouses initially resist my attempts to interpret their talk, because by and large, both men and women expect their spouses to talk in their language. For example, a wife who is pushing her husband to talk more about his feelings might say "Why are you holding back? I know there are feelings in there somewhere." Her husband might respond with "Not any I can't handle. I don't need to spill all my feelings out."

Each spouse is judging the other based on the assumption that his or her language is the correct one. She's saying "What's wrong with you? Why won't you talk about your feelings? He retorts, "What's wrong with you? Why do you talk about your feelings?" In my experience, feelings of insecurity lurk behind every accusation that someone is wrong. I keep that in mind when I reword the conversation. I encourage couples to *listen* to each other instead of criticizing each other and *hear* what their spouse is saying from their spouse's perspective. Here's how I'd translate their conversation:

The wife: Why are you holding back? I know there are feelings in there somewhere.
Translation: I worry that you don't love me and that I must be doing something wrong because you aren't opening up to me in the way I want you to.

Her husband: Not any I can't handle. I don't need to spill all my feelings out.
Translation: I'm afraid to open up because you'll think I'm weak and can't handle my own problems.

When your husband seems impassive or quiet or he resists talking to you, your feelings may be hurt and you may wonder what you're doing wrong. Out of anger, hurt, or frustration, it's easy to fall back into stereotypes and cliches rather than trying to understand that your husband has a valid but *different* point of view. You may be tempted to dismiss him with statements like "He's an emotional wasteland" or "He wouldn't know a feeling if it came up and bit him." But as this book will show, your husband has plenty of feelings, and he's probably frustrated that you don't understand him. This book will help you to learn about his feelings as well as to respect and appreciate— rather than fear or dismiss—the differences between you.

Only recently have couples even tried to talk to each other and work toward having intimate relationships. In the past, marriage was a contract—primarily for having children. Spouses had specific, well-defined roles. Now all that's changed, and for the first time in our cultural history, both men and women want to achieve closeness with their spouses. It's an enormous change, and it's not easy. We're really not geared up as a society for this sort of union. It's tough being pioneers.

If you want your marriage to be a partnership, remember that it's not about pushing your agenda or your husband pushing his. Talking about what concerns you—whether it's sex, money, the kids, or who vacuumed the rug last—requires compromise and negotiation. Chances are you learned how to talk to your husband from your mother. A lot of what you learned will have to be unlearned, because very few of our parents knew the arts of talking and arguing *well.*

I believe that if you tell your husband what you want *in a way that he can hear,* he will be more than willing to do what's being asked of him. But you have to be reasonable about what you expect from him. For example, if he's not accustomed to talking about his feelings, then expecting him to talk to you in the same way that you would talk to a woman friend is unreasonable and unfair. I often have to remind my women clients that although they may have had a lifetime of sharing feelings, thoughts, and problems, their husbands have had a lifetime of keeping their thoughts and feelings to themselves.

My goal in couples therapy is to get husbands and wives to talk and listen to each other, ask questions, and probe each other's reasoning and feelings—in other words, to get to know each other. It's a constant source of amazement for me that women who have been married for years and who swear they know their husbands inside and out don't really know them at all, having pigeonholed them as emotional dwarfs, insensitive fathers, or sex maniacs.

You can learn a more effective way of talking to your husband. By framing your conversation so that he will listen and understand, you make it possible for him to respond to you in the ways you would like. And when you are able to talk to your husband in an open manner, you will get to know him and he you.

About the Book

How to Talk to Your Husband/How to Talk to Your Wife is designed to supply you with the tools you need to talk to each other. It will help you bridge not only the gender gap but your personal differences in a practical, no-nonsense way.

The chapter titles are the same on both sides of the book and cover what I consider the major trouble spots in marriage: intimacy, kids, money, sex, and daily life. Within each chapter I've included several of the most common complaints, concerns, and difficulties and offered several alternative ways to talk about these issues with your husband or respond to his discussions with you.

Intimacy

Both men and women want intimate relationships. But your husband's brand of intimacy may be different from yours. For example, he may feel close to you just hanging out, watching TV together, whereas you're more likely to want some conversation.

Chances are your husband doesn't have the *need* to talk—about feelings, random thoughts, problems—to the extent that you do in order to feel close. Because of these differences, women often find themselves pushing husbands to talk more about feelings than the husbands are comfortable doing. In Chapter 1, "Intimacy," you will learn how to talk to your husband about your feelings so that he will listen. You will also learn how to encourage your husband to tell you what he would like in order to feel closer to you.

Kids

Raising children can be one of the most joyful parts of a marriage. It can also be one of the most troubling. Child rearing is like religion and politics: everybody has strong opinions about it and tends to think their way is the right way. Spouses often disagree about how much nurturing or discipline a child should have—and about who should be providing it. In Chapter 2, "Kids," you'll learn to talk with your husband about sharing the work of child rearing and the problems of discipline versus nurturing. Recent studies show that men and women do parent their children differently. Talking about your differences in a mature, productive way is essential to the health of your relationship.

Money

And then, of course, there's money. Who earns it, saves it, or spends it and on what is the source of constant bickering in many marriages. Money means different things to different people. For instance, to your husband, how much money he makes might be related to his feelings of self-worth. For you, money might represent security, good schools for the kids, and some nice vacations. If you sense that your husband's ego is involved in money, it might make talking about it difficult. Chapter 3, "Money," tells you how to go about discussing this sensitive topic and how to get your point across without making your husband feel defensive or inadequate.

Sex

Most people feel vulnerable about their sexuality. Both men and women can be hurt by an unkind comment about performance or attractiveness. But sometimes sex just isn't working right. Chapter 4, "Sex," examines ways to talk about such sensitive topics as sexual performance. You will learn new methods besides the "I have a headache" routine or pretending to be asleep to tell your husband No if you're not in the mood. And Yes!, you can find the words to comfortably tell him what you like, what you don't like, and when.

Daily Life

Along with all these problems, you and your husband have to deal with simply living together day by day. The minor problems that arise every day take on greater significance if you don't discuss them. Many couples spend years of their lives living in a world of low-grade tension because of everyday irritations that don't get resolved. Because you probably never learned how to have a good fight, you may feel this tension is preferable to letting your husband have it when he doesn't do his share of household chores. Discover in Chapter 5, "Daily Life," how to talk about such things as who does the housework, how to handle moodiness, and how not to get stuck having the same old arguments all the time.

How to Use This Book

You can use this book in one of two ways: If you're feeling ambitious, read through the entire thing (both sides) and then reread a particular scenario when that problem comes up for you.

If you're pressed for time, look up a particular problem and save the rest of the book for later. For instance, if you're having a hard time getting your husband to spend time with the kids or if you want him to share more of the household chores, go directly to page 21 "He doesn't spend enough time with the kids," or page 73, "I do most of the work." Also, read the corresponding chapter on your husband's side of the book to get a feeling for what he may be experiencing.

The Big Picture

Learning productive ways to talk to your husband will help you in *all* of your relationships. For instance, you may be able to learn from your husband how to conduct more solution-oriented discussions or how to be more direct in certain settings.

You and your husband are part of a revolution. For the first time men and women are struggling to get to know each other in ways they never did before. At the same time, both sexes are feeling freer to express all parts of themselves and refusing to limit themselves to "male" and "female" responses and roles. *How to Talk to Your Husband/How to Talk to Your Wife* will help both you and your husband achieve the closeness and partnership that you want.

Trouble Spot One:
Intimacy

For many women intimacy *is* talking. When you're talking to your husband about your day, the kids, work, or what happened to your next-door neighbor's cat, you feel close to him. If your husband gives you his full attention, listens to what you have to say, and responds with some experiences of his own, you're in heaven. Intimacy is about connecting and sharing feelings, ideas, and physical affection. If you're having a hard time, you want your husband to comfort you. Likewise, if your husband is in pain, you want to comfort him. Not only do you want this kind of intimacy, you probably feel that it's essential to a good relationship and the more of it, the better. You may even gauge your self-worth by how intimate your relationship with your husband is. If so, you may be tempted to push your husband into giving you what you want or what you think you're supposed to have rather than respecting his need for space.

A lot of talking may have an effect on your husband that is opposite of the effect it has on you. In other words, for you it can be an aphrodisiac, for him a turn-off. No matter how close to you your husband feels, he will still protect his private time and space. Your husband, like most people, likes to feel independent, and sometimes your need to talk may seem like an intrusion to him. If you are focused on getting the most intimacy possible from your husband, you may misinterpret his normal pattern of intimacy followed by a bid for independence. If you misread his need for space as a lack of love for you, you may get hurt or angry and demanding. You may even feel like a failure and get angry with yourself, which is likely to make you try harder. But if all your husband is looking for is a bit of time alone, then these reactions from you will elicit exactly the behavior you feared initially—withdrawal.

Men often see the need for intimacy as a "female thing" and something to be held in check. When you pressure your husband to talk, share feelings, or cuddle, he may feel overwhelmed by what he sees as your neediness. The solution is to back off a little. Let him come to you even if you have to wait longer than is comfortable for you.

Many men don't readily seek out others for closeness or comfort; a man's tendency is to tough it out alone. Men have been taught to depend on themselves, so their needs for intimacy are often different from yours. When you ask your husband to talk about his feelings, your request may be met with a mixture of confusion and resentment or a simple "Everything's fine." If you push him for more, he may decide that he can't satisfy you because you want something from him that he doesn't understand or that doesn't come naturally to him.

If you're worried that you're doing something wrong because your husband is not as intimate with you as you think he should be, it's a good time to look at the differences in your *comfort zones,* that is, how much contact and talking you each like to have with others. A good way to do this is by observing your friendships and your husband's. Friendships between women usually involve sharing confidences and giving mutual support through talking and listening, maybe with some hugs thrown in. Close friendships between men are often centered around playing or watching sports or playing cards or other games, all things that require little talking or sharing of feelings. But many men would argue that sitting side by side with a buddy watching the Lakers massacre the Bulls is just as intimate as the long conversations their wives have with their friends around the kitchen table or on the phone.

Men often don't attach their feelings of self-worth to establishing intimate relationships the way women do. In fact, some men go out of their way to appear not to establish a close relationship with their wives. You and your women friends may admire or envy a woman who has a close relationship with her husband. To you, she is successful. Men, on the other hand, look upon intimacy with suspicion and tease each other about it. If a man has a close relationship with his wife, he is not as likely to discuss it with his friends as his wife is.

Many men separate sex from intimacy, which really riles the women in their lives. It's difficult for most women to have sex without feeling close. But men can have sex without attaching feelings of intimacy—that's why men more often say that a casual sexual encounter means nothing, a claim women simply don't believe. If you and your husband view sex and intimacy differently, you may often find yourselves at cross-purposes. Does your husband want to have sex right after an argument? For him, sex is a perfect way to make up. For you, sex is something that happens *after* you've made up—so you interpret his sexual advances to mean that he's discounting your feelings.

Working toward greater intimacy with your husband means expressing what you need in a way that your husband can hear and also understanding and respecting his point of view. Since your ego is involved, you will have to be alert to your feelings of panic, worthlessness, and failure if you don't achieve what you feel is an intimate relationship.

In my book, watching a football game together doesn't qualify as intimacy.

Don't be so quick to dismiss your husband's brand of intimacy. Yes, it's different from yours, but if you expect him to give you what you need, you must also be willing to see that his needs are equally valid.

Some of the most memorable times your husband has had may have occurred in front of the television with a bunch of guys, watching a great play-off game or final. Men attach themselves to teams in ways that most women do not. They identify with the players and the coaches. They call out plays, scream out their frustrations, and deliver their criticisms with no mercy. Men are elated when their team wins and depressed when it loses. If you can talk sports with your husband, you will be a part of his experience and he will feel closer to you.

Try sitting down with him now and then to watch a

game of tennis, basketball, or football. Once you figure out what's going on, you may actually enjoy it. The two of you can pick opposing teams and bet against each other. Whoever wins owes the other a dinner (this is where you get your needs met). Or, pick the same team and rejoice (or get depressed) together.

If you don't want to join in, back off and let your husband enjoy himself. Don't spoil his pleasure by nagging him ("You see your friends more than I see you"), vying for his attention ("I'm not slamming dishes around—I'm cleaning the cupboards"), or being sarcastic ("When you find your missing chromosome, you won't be so obsessed with sports").

None of these behaviors will get you what you want. Your husband will either go to another part of the house or to someone else's house to watch sports. If you really lay it on thick and manage to make him feel guilty, he will turn off the TV, but he will resent you for it and withdraw from you in other ways.

If your husband watches more sports than the average male—more than just one night a week or both Saturday and Sunday, let's say—you could do one or more of the following:

- Suggest a walk, breakfast, or an early dinner for the two of you before the game begins.
- Make plans to be with a friend during the game. Go for a jog, shopping, or lunch.
- Discuss a compromise with your husband. For instance, ask him to choose one night or two that the two of you spend together. This way he can peruse the sports schedule and make some decisions about which games are most important.

5

- Be positive and upbeat when you talk to your husband, not disapproving and resentful.

He listens to my feelings but doesn't share his feelings with me.

Your husband might be perfectly willing to listen to you because he sees your desire to talk as proof that you need him. He might even get satisfaction from being strong for you. However, in order to share his feelings, he must be vulnerable, a trait many men don't associate with maleness. That he be vulnerable is the opposite of what he thinks you're asking of him. When you ask him to listen, he thinks you want him to solve your problem or be strong for you.

Let's look again at friendships between men. Unlike women, most men don't talk as openly about their feelings with their male friends. If a man does discuss his feelings or a problem he's having on the homefront with a male friend, both men are likely to be embarrassed. To them, it seems clear he can't work it out for himself—or else he wouldn't be talking about it. Being unable to solve one's own problems is a sign of weakness to most men. So a good friend's response will probably be along the lines of "Well, you can handle it" or "It sounds like that's under control," and then one of them will change the subject. This response allows your husband to avoid the "one down" feeling he has when he talks about a problem.

When your husband doesn't share his feelings with you, try not to take it personally. Remember that sharing feelings is not as easy for him as it is for you and that he may need some help.

If your husband listens to you with interest, consider it an act of love. He is giving you his undivided attention. Tell him you appreciate his listening. After you're done talking, don't say "So, how do you feel?" This will put him on the spot, and he won't know how to begin. Give him a hand. Ask him questions. Has he ever had a similar experience? Has he ever felt the way you just described? How would he react in the same situation?

If he answers with a simple yes or no, then go further. Say

- Oh, so you felt similar to me? Your feelings would have been hurt too, then?
- You don't get hurt the way I do. I guess we're different that way. Why doesn't that kind of thing bother you much?

The idea is to repeat back what your husband said with a little variation, and then ask for more information. This is called "reflective listening"; it's effective in many situations.

If you're accustomed to the give and take of women talking to each other, reflective listening may seem condescending or simplistic, but it is not. It's a tool that therapists, parents, couples, and friends use, usually with good results. Your husband will appreciate your help and eventually offer his feelings without prompting.

If he is still reluctant to share his feelings with you, consider whether you are putting him off in some way. When he doesn't comply with your request or answers with a simple yes or no, do you throw up your hands and walk away? Tell him he doesn't love you or that he's a neanderthal? Get hurt and pout? Accuse him of withholding?

Instead, say something like

- I'd like to hear what you're feeling when you're ready.
- When you don't tell me how you're feeling, I think there's something wrong with me. Is there something I'm doing that makes you uncomfortable?

Then, listen to what he says. When your husband does share his feelings with you, no matter how minute, don't criticize, belittle, or dismiss him. Men often feel they're at a disadvantage when it comes to talking about feelings; women do it so well and with such ease that it can be intimidating. One good way to insure that your husband isn't under the impression that there is one right way to express feelings is to accept his feelings in whatever form they emerge.

When I talk about my feelings, he criticizes me for being too needy.

Instead of listening, does your husband get annoyed and critical? Does he say things like "Can't you just take care of it?" or "Why do you have to tell me every little thing?" Has he ever walked out of the room saying "What the hell do you want from me?"

If this is going on in your household, your husband is probably overwhelmed by what he considers your neediness. This could be happening for a number of reasons, but first let's look at your behavior.

Do you do any of the following?

- bombard him with your feelings the minute he walks in the door

8

- ignore the signals that he needs space, such as his turning on the TV or getting fidgety
- cling to him when he says he wants to go out or just to another room

If you recognize your own behavior here, you need to pull back and give your husband some breathing room. If you don't read or respect his signals, your husband will resent you for what he perceives as your efforts to keep him from being independent. One of the ways he is trying to ward you off is by criticizing you. He might say "You're never satisfied" or "Am I going to have to peel you off of me?" Here are some suggestions:

- If your husband leaves the room, don't follow him.
- If he says he needs some peace and quiet, don't argue; let him have it.
- Don't give in to the impulse to cling, physically or emotionally.
- Make plans to spend time with friends or doing your own activities in order to give him some space.

Your husband might be feeling overwhelmed because he doesn't understand what you expect of him or know how to give you what you want. Men are solution-oriented. Perhaps he feels responsible for solving your problems and feels that you are disappointed in him. In this case he may criticize you to cover up his own feelings of inadequacy. If this sounds right, try being more specific. Say "I'd like five minutes of your time so I can bitch and moan about my mother. Is now okay? If not, when?" Don't exceed the time. When the five minutes are up, thank him for listening. Or say "I'd like a couple of hugs. I've had a crummy day." Don't ask for a hug if your husband is already in a state of withdrawal. If you get your hugs, thank him, but *don't* start to talk about your feelings. The point is to stick to your original request.

If your husband still criticizes you for being needy, say

- What am I doing that's making you uncomfortable?
- What can I do differently?
- It sounds like you don't like my asking you to listen. Can you tell me why not?
- Can you be specific about what you're angry about?

If your husband continues to push you away and no amount of trying on your part seems to help, then you're dealing with either his excessive fear of closeness or his still-raw feelings of being overwhelmed. In either case, give him time to approach you. It may take a while, but if he is given the space to feel comfortable, it will occur.

I want intimacy, he wants sex.

Men often don't distinguish sex from intimacy. If you hug and kiss your husband, sit on his lap, or massage his shoulders, chances are he will think and act "sex." If you feel sad your husband might hold you, but even in the midst of your tears, his holding might shift from affectionate to sexual. Many women feel enraged, offended, or mistreated when their husbands misread their intent. But don't yield to the temptation to say "All you ever think about is sex," "You don't care about my feelings," or "God, you're such an insensitive jerk." Chances are your husband is not trying to hurt or demean you, he is simply responding to what his body and mind are telling him. If your husband doesn't make a distinction between affection and comforting and sex, then you need to be in charge of what you want and learn to communicate it to him.

If you want cuddling and you know your husband will respond sexually, then be clear and say what you want beforehand:

- I'm really upset about my boss; I'd like some TLC.
- I'm crazy about you; let me give you a big smooch.
- I'm feeling sad. Would you hold me?
- You've had a bad day. I want to give you a hug.

If your husband doesn't understand, add a blunt statement such as "And I don't want it to turn into sex" or "And sex isn't what I'm looking for right now."

Many wives get angry at their husbands for "not listening" to their request for nonsexual affection. These women feel they are coerced into having sex. It's your job to request what you want and follow through. If you give in to your husband so as not to "disappoint him" or "make him angry," then you are part of the problem. If after you tell your husband what you want his response turns sexual and you go for it, don't expect him to listen to you or believe you the next time.

It is also your responsibility to keep your own behavior in check. If you touch your husband in a sexual way after you've said that all you want is closeness, you're being unfair and you're expecting too much from him. Don't be a tease.

If you change your mind about having sex, wait. Thank him for comforting you, and later—it doesn't have to be too long—initiate sex. If you don't separate the two, as you asked your husband to do, he will probably be confused. Also, the next time you request affection, he will be hopeful that you will get turned on again.

11

If your husband has agreed ahead of time to give you some nonsexual affection but then becomes sexual with you, say

- We agreed not to be sexual.
- This doesn't feel comfortable to me.
- Take your hand off my breast (please).

Continue to be clear and let him know how important it is to you that he follow through with what he promised. If he tells you that it's impossible for him to control his sexual feelings, call him on it. Say "Of course you can control your sexual feelings. What you're really saying is that you don't want to. It's important to me that you put aside your sexual feelings when I just want to be held. I have to trust that you can do that for me."

After a while, your husband will begin to enjoy the benefits of hugs and kisses. He can then ask *you* for affection knowing that he can feel your warmth and love without any demands.

Whenever I try to get close to him, he changes the subject or makes a joke.

Men often change the subject when talking to each other, especially when one of them has talked about an important or painful feeling. To a man this is a sign of respect, much like saying "I know you can handle this; there's no need to talk about it anymore." Women, on the other hand, respond to a friend's feelings by talking about their own similar experiences. If you feel hurt when your husband responds to you as he would to his friends, it's because you expect him to react as *your* friends would. You may be convinced that your husband doesn't respect your feelings or isn't listening, but it's possible that he's simply trying to reassure you that he thinks you are in control and that you are capable, which is what he would want from you if he were in a similar position. It's also possible that he is uncomfortable with your desire for closeness so he's not able to relax. If your husband isn't as accustomed to closeness as you are, he might get fidgety, make a joke, or ignore you as a way of coping with his own feelings of discomfort or to push you away so he can return to a safer, more familiar distance.

Since you are asking your husband to change his behavior, behavior that he's probably never questioned and that works just fine with his friends, you will have to be patient. Your husband's responses won't change overnight, and the changes will come in small doses. You can goose him along a bit by having a few friendly reactions to his behavior:

- When he listens *even briefly,* comment on it. "Thanks for listening" is sufficient—don't belabor the point.
- When he changes the subject yet again, go with it, then circle back to what you were talking about. You can say "To get back to what I was saying earlier . . ." or something to that effect.
- If you tell him your feelings at a particular moment and he makes a joke, laugh. Don't get stiff and resentful. Your husband may be trying to make you smile.
- If you're not in the mood for jokes or subject changes and you really want to talk, ask him if another time

would be better. Don't hound him, but don't let him off the hook either.

Sometimes women choose a reticent man and then do everything in their power to change him into someone else. In couples therapy, many spouses discover—to their dismay—that the very attributes that attracted them to each other are the ones that they later have problems with or want to change. If this is the case, it's time for you to look at your own choices and realize that perhaps you are expecting too much from your husband. Instead, concentrate on the traits your husband has that you already find delightful. Start accepting who he is, not who you want to make him into.

Many women who are afraid of closeness themselves get involved with men who are distant. You pursue, he runs away, and you're both unhappy. You blame your husband ("He won't let me get close to him"); he blames you ("She's always coming after me"). But it's a joint problem: you're both afraid of closeness. The best way to figure out whether you fit into this category is to see what happens if your husband makes overtures to *you*—when he stops running. Do you panic? Do you withdraw? Do you subtly criticize his attempt to be close to you? If so, work on changing your own behavior. Notice when you are pushing your husband away with an angry or critical remark or by withdrawing. Work up to owning up to it by apologizing or simply stating what you've observed about your own behavior.

The sudden urge you feel to make a phone call or to weed your garden when your husband makes a stab at closeness is equivalent to his jokes and subject changes.

Instead try sitting quietly and receiving his overture. Initially you'll feel anxious, but in time it will get easier.

I can't get him to talk about his day.

When everything is going fine, most men don't feel a need to talk about their day. And if something is amiss, many men won't talk about it until they have a clue about how they can fix it. Don't be surprised if in answer to your question "How was your day?" your husband says "Fine" or "I fixed the Reynolds account." Chances are you didn't know the Reynolds account needed fixing. However, if you ask your husband any more questions about it, he's likely to react as if you want to talk about ancient history.

You, on the other hand, probably like to talk about many aspects of your day: the people, the problems, the embarrassing moment in front of your boss. It makes you feel close to your husband when you can share what happened while you weren't together.

If you think your husband would like to say more about his day but it doesn't flow naturally, ask specific questions:

- Did Jody get her raise?
- Did your staff talk about the earthquake in Guatemala?
- Did Mary have her baby?
- What kinds of projects are you working on this week?
- How's Old Man Reynolds?

There's nothing to be gained from trying to force your husband to talk about his day if he doesn't want to. If he doesn't respond well to your questions—gets tense or annoyed or gives one-word answers—then you're defeating your purpose of being closer to him by continuing to ask. Talk about your day. Tell him it's relaxing for you to do so, but don't expect him to reciprocate.

Sometimes people just want to come home, relax, and forget about their day at work. Rehashing it makes them unable to relax. If this is so for your husband, suggest going for a walk before dinner or taking your drinks onto the patio. Remember that intimacy is what you're looking for. It may show up in a different form, but it's intimacy nonetheless. Sitting quietly can be as intimate as talking, especially if your husband finds it a pleasurable way to unwind from the day.

Your husband may find it relaxing to come home and flip on the news. Many women complain about this behavior. If you push your husband, he may turn off the TV, but he'll resent you for trying to control him. Rather than taking his interest in the news as a personal affront, consider sitting down with him and finding out what's been going on around the world. Or busy yourself with some other activity and allow him to unwind in his own way, at his own pace. Chances are, after he's checked in and made sure nothing much has changed since the last time he looked, he will be in a better, more relaxed mood and ready to talk with you.

Trouble Spot Two:
Kids

Rarely do two people agree completely on how to raise kids. So talking about your kids with your husband, especially when there's a problem, gets frustrating fast. Your husband's parenting style, expectations of your children, and way of communicating with them may all be different from yours. If you, like many women, spend more time with the kids than your husband and do more of the work of child rearing, you may find it especially hard to listen to what he has to say about them. After all, who knows more about your kids than you do?

Instead of feeling guilty for not spending more time with the children, however, your husband may feel that you spend too much time with them. Instead of appreciating your hard work, does your husband complain that you don't make time for him, that you're more interested in the kids than in him, or that you don't make love anymore? Do you snap back that if he spent less time in front of the TV, and more time helping with the kids, maybe you could pick yourself up off the floor and drag yourself to bed occasionally? Many couples play out one version of this argument or another day after day. Like as not, he walks away feeling attacked, and you walk away feeling abused.

This pattern is at the root of many couples' arguments regarding kids but is actually a relationship problem. For instance, it might be easier for both you and your husband to focus on the kids rather than to talk about whether you are getting your own emotional needs met. If you have difficulty expressing feelings directly, as many couples do, it's tempting to submerge the real problem and talk about it *through* another issue. But since the real issue, let's say intimacy, is never addressed, it's never resolved.

When couples are more direct in saying what they feel, their conflicts over spending time together versus spending time with the kids disappears. For instance, if your husband were to say "I miss you," "I'm feeling left out," or "Let's make a date and go out to dinner, just the two of us," you might react differently. And if you talk to your husband about wanting more help or support in a way that he can *hear*—not in an argument and not as a way to punish him when he wants something from you—he might respond positively.

Another set of problems has to do with the differences in the ways you and your husband feel are "right" for raising your kids. This can be traced back to your upbringing. The way you were brought up influences the way you raise your own children. You either agree with your parents' parenting—let's say the way they disciplined you—and do it the same way, or you disagree and make absolutely sure you do it differently. Either way, you have an opinion about what's right in this regard. And depending on how your husband was raised, he too will have his own opinion on this same issue.

Many couples have ongoing arguments about discipline, rules, allowances, and privileges. Maybe you're more lenient and your husband more of a disciplinarian. These differences, even if slight, can become magnified during a disagreement. Soon your husband is telling you your kid is going to be a criminal because you're not teaching him limits, and you're screaming that your husband is a Nazi.

Because you have strong feelings about how kids should be raised, you may not be willing to compromise with your husband. But regarding issues other than nonnegotiable things like child abuse, neglect, criticism—in other words, destructive ways of parenting—and some rules and regulations, there is lots of room for variation. Let's say your husband wants your two-year-old daughter, Mary, not to throw her food on the floor. But every time he feeds Mary you say "You're restricting her" and try to take over. Your husband continues feeding Mary but says through gritted teeth that you let the kid get away with murder. A solution to this problem is that you and your husband take turns feeding Mary, each in your own way. Mary learns to eat one way with Daddy and another way with Mommy; it's a simple adjustment for her. When you discover that Mary does just fine with both of you, you realize that there is more than one way (yours) to raise a kid.

It is not uncommon for women to feel responsible for their children's emotional well-being as well as their physical well-being. Sometimes this means you see your own husband as the enemy. For example, you overhear your husband talking to your son about his grades in a voice you find to be a little too critical or loud. Convinced that your husband does not match you in the nurturing or sensitivity department, you think your child will be damaged, and you may feel compelled to move in to protect him. However, if you intervene, you embarrass your husband and take away any authority he has with the children. In the process you ally yourself with the children against him. Since your husband may not have been trained to pick up on the nuances of feelings and behavior in the same way you were, he's going to end up feeling like he can't do anything right. These reactions lead to more and more distance and misunderstanding between you and your husband.

Your kids will develop a separate relationship with their father, something you should not interfere with unless he is being abusive. Current research suggests that there are gender differences in parenting styles and that kids benefit from both styles. The argument goes that kids don't need two mommies, they need a mommy and a daddy. Each contributes something different and valuable. So, while accepting behavior from your husband that you don't like is hard, it's in your children's best interest to do so. Other studies show, for instance, that boys who are raised with mothers only are far more aggressive than boys who are raised with a father in the home. So your husband must be doing something right!

In this chapter you'll find discussions of some of the problems that wives have with their husbands, along with some suggestions on how to talk to your husband about them.

He doesn't spend enough time with the kids.

In order to deal with this complaint, it's a good idea to figure out how "pure" it is. Are you complaining solely about the time your husband spends with the kids, or is his lack of time spent with you included as well? If you want your husband to spend time with you, that's a separate problem. Don't lump yourself in with the kids.

If you think that true love and family bliss requires that you and your husband stop any outside activity and he hasn't done that, then no amount of time he spends with the children will suffice. If you think that every time he goes out with a friend or plays a weekend tennis game he's deserting the family, it's you who is being unreasonable and unfair. And if you keep saying things like "Your son wanted to show you his science project, but of course you weren't around" or talking about how selfish your husband is, you're not likely to solve this problem.

While it's true that some men don't spend enough time with their children, it's also true that some women spend too much. If you are sacrificing your free time to your children, then so be it, but don't resent your husband for not doing the same. If your husband is making time to see friends, he's a good example for you of how to balance your own life better. Ask him to care for the kids one night while you go out with a friend, to the library, or for a drive to the beach. If you take time for yourself, your resentment will lessen.

Maybe your husband isn't spending time with the kids because he's not comfortable with them. He may be at a loss as to what to do. Lots of men want to be more involved with their kids but don't know where to start; they feel like they're "all thumbs." To him, it may seem that everything runs so smoothly without him: the kids come to you with their skinned knees and problems with their friends, they ask your permission to go out after school, and you hand out allowances every week. He might not realize that the kids miss him or would like him to contribute more to the family. Give him a hand. Let him know he's important to the kids. Don't say "Spencer grew two inches since you last saw him." Say "Spencer really likes spending time with you." Here are some suggestions to help your husband get involved:

- Ask your husband to do specific things with the kids. For instance, say "Would you help Susie with her batting practice?" or "Greg's having a tough time with polynomials. Would you check his homework for the next few days?"
- Plan activities for the whole family. Play games after dinner, have a lively discussion—husband included. Or plan something that your husband enjoys and that he can share with the children—fishing, some sporting event, or a museum.
- Include him in decision making. Let's say your ten-year-old son asks your permission to go to a Grateful Dead concert. Instead of shrieking "Where did we go wrong?!" or volunteering your old tie-dyed T-shirt, turn to your husband and ask him what he thinks.

If your husband does the yard work or likes puttering in the garage, suggest that the kids follow him around for a while. If you think he spends too much time watching TV or playing with his computer, negotiate with him. Say "You spend four hours every night watching the tube/playing with the computer. How about if you put aside an hour of that time for the kids?" Encourage him to spend time teaching the children about computers or watching a children's show on television.

If your goal is to get your husband to spend time with the kids, don't complain about what he does with them. In other words, if he wants to take them to a baseball game, don't say "Well, I was hoping you would show Danny how to do long division today."

If he says that he's already spending all his free time with the kids, that he's working 75 hours a week *for the kids*, or that you're too demanding, ask him to be specific about the time he's spending with the kids. You may have to explain that sleeping under the same roof doesn't count as spending time with the kids. Discuss—in an interested, not hostile, way—what kind of role model your husband's father was. Have a discussion about priorities. You might want to tell him that although you appreciate his efforts to provide financially for his family, you would prefer that he be home rather than out working so hard to bring home extra bucks.

He's too impatient/critical.

It's possible your husband has no idea what effect he's having on the children when he raises his voice or is critical. Sometimes just your talking to him and telling him how he's coming across can enlighten him, and he may then elicit your help in changing his behavior.

More often, however, the problem is a difference in parenting styles and sometimes a gender difference. Men tend to focus on their children's performance; women, more on their children's emotional life. Sometimes it might seem to you that your husband is expecting too much from the children, but research shows that children benefit from both a father's focus on more concrete issues like grades and winning in sports and a mother's focus on feelings. Your husband is focused on your kids' future; he worries about how his children are going to cope in the big, bad world. He feels it's his job to toughen them up.

Your husband may be proudest of your son when he wins at tennis or some other sport. You, on the other hand, may feel happiest when he volunteers to help his younger sister with her homework or mows the lawn for the old lady next door. While your husband may feel that he doesn't want the kids to grow up too "soft," you may feel that any demands for improvement are detrimental to your children's self-esteem. Take a closer look. If you are expecting your husband to be like you and to treat the kids the way you do (with the same sensitivity) perhaps you're not being fair to your husband or the kids.

Whenever your child is hurt, it hurts you. So it's difficult when you think that your husband is hurting your child's feelings with his tone of voice or his insensitivity. If you think your husband is being too harsh, tell him. You can also give him vent for his frustration. For instance, if you know your teenage daughter Linda is driving him crazy with her incessant rages, her outlandish hair, and her hours on the telephone every night, acknowledge it. Give your husband a chance to complain to you about it without your judging him.

If you notice that your children are having negative reactions to your husband, such as tears, anger, and hurt feelings, tell him. Don't say "You're too critical." Instead, say "When you called Claire your little pudgy baby, it hurt her feelings." Be concrete. If your husband disagrees with you or says you're being critical of him, suggest that he talk to Claire.

If the kids complain to you about their father, encourage them to talk with him about their feelings. Then tell your husband what your children's concerns are and suggest that he talk to them. Your husband may be uncomfortable in this role, so ask him if he wants your help in opening a conversation. If so, consider that a good way to go about creating a dialogue is to start having family meetings perhaps once a week. Set a specific time every week for the entire family to get together and talk about *whatever* they want. Two kids might complain about each other, or you might talk about the chores for the week and how they were handled. Talk about your feelings and encourage your children to talk about theirs. This is when the issues about your husband's parenting will come up. Since everyone is talking about their feelings about everybody else, your husband isn't singled out.

Don't back down from this problem or give up talking about it. If your husband's criticism or impatience is having an impact on the children's self-esteem, you have to keep at it.

I say no, he says yes.

If your husband doesn't participate much in raising the children, he may feel he has to make it up to the children by being the good guy. Of course, your kids' radar will pick this up, and they will bypass you to get to Dad. You will feel undermined and furious with your husband when your son triumphantly announces that he is spending the night at his friend's house—even though you said no an hour ago—because Dad said he could.

It's important to get at your husband's reasons for this behavior because it may be a symptom of other problems in your relationship. For instance, if your husband is angry at you because you are ignoring him or are critical of him, he may find that making alliances with his kids against you is an effective way to punish you. On the other hand, your husband may be saying yes to certain things because the two of you disagree about what's permissible and what's not. Is he saying yes to the kids because the first thing that pops out of your mouth is no? If your husband tells you you're too negative, pay attention to your own voice and reactions to the kids. If you discover that he's right, you may be unconsciously repeating some parenting behavior that you learned from your parents. Ask your husband to help you by pointing out times when you shoot from the lip.

Discuss the problem with your husband directly. Ask him if something else is bothering him. Tell him you notice his behavior and it's undermining your relationships with him and the children. Suggest that you both sit down and discuss how you will handle this problem in the future. Tell him it's important that you present a united front to the children and that the two of you need to work as a team. To do that, you both need to do the following:

- Discuss your children's requests before saying yes or no. Say, "Your dad/mom and I will discuss it and let you know."

- Agree on what you will tell them.
- Stick to what you agreed upon.

If there are serious differences in what you and your husband think is permissible, it's time to hammer them out. You have to be willing to compromise and negotiate. Unless there are underlying power struggles going on, you will be able to talk through this problem.

If the problem continues, don't let him waffle out of what he's doing by saying things like "Well, it was just this time" or "Why are you making such a big deal about it?" Keep insisting that you follow the teamwork approach as described in this section, and call him on it each time he says yes when you've said no.

If the kids act up, he blames me.

If your husband seems to expect you to do the job of raising the kids yet criticizes your efforts, you're going to feel enraged and undermined. This is a familiar pattern with couples. When you're feeling angry and betrayed, it's hard to step back and examine the possible reasons for your husband's behavior, but let's give it a whirl.

It's possible your husband feels left out. Perhaps you're excluding your husband from your private relationship with your kids. If you are "in the know" with your kids and don't include your husband in some of their shenanigans, instead of telling you he feels like a third wheel in his own house, he's likely to strike out at you. Don't have private jokes with your kids or give a knowing wink to certain behaviors that your husband is in the

27

dark about. Your husband is your partner, your kids aren't. For women who feel they are not getting certain emotional needs met from their husband, it's sometimes tempting to form alliances with their kids. If this is the case, you need to address your problems with your husband directly. If you want more affection from him or time with him, say so.

Another reason your husband might be critical of you is because he feels inadequate as a parent. If he feels like you do everything right and he does everything wrong, he may not feel comfortable asking for help. Instead he may find reason to complain about you. Check your behavior to see if you could be contributing to those feelings. For instance, do you make fun of his bumbling attempts to change diapers or to "be there" emotionally for his little girl? Be more supportive of your husband's efforts at parenting and he will be less critical of you.

Perhaps your husband is angry at you about something completely unrelated to the children but focuses on their behavior. If this is the case, this problem goes beyond the children and is more directly connected to your spousal relationship. Confront your husband. "If you're angry about something, I'd like to know about it directly."

Maybe your children are spoiled. Perhaps you are too lenient, and the children have no structure. If this is true, you and your husband need to sit down and discuss some middle ground for parenting. Ask for his help if you have trouble disciplining the children or saying no. In other words, don't resist your husband, embrace his loving attempts to help.

If your husband worries about what people will think

every time your two-year-old throws a typical tantrum, then it's probably more comfortable for him to blame you than the child. He probably feels helpless in the face of your child's behavior. This is a good time to talk about what can normally be expected from a child at certain ages. Chances are you have read more baby and child behavior books than your husband. You can suggest (probably again) that he read a few, or you can simply say "Well, the Penelope Leach book says that this is typical behavior." Or say "That bothered me too until I read that it's completely normal."

Still, your husband may continue to blame you. Let's take a look at what you might be doing that contributes to the problem. Do you assume control of the children or make sure he doesn't spend equal time with them?

You need to let go of the kids a little and let your husband participate. You might feel you know best and constantly intervene because he inadvertantly hurts your kids' feelings. Let him have his relationship with his children without constant criticism from you. Your children will adjust to his imperfections. Keeping your husband from interacting with the kids out of a need to "protect" them will harm both the kids' relationship with their father and your relationship with your husband.

Include your husband in the decisions you make about your kids. Discuss their behavior with him and ask him for his opinion. Decide what issues are important. Insist on being a team. If he continues to blame you for your children's behavior, you can either ignore him or call him on it every time. Whichever response you choose, be consistent. You can then also take credit for how well your children turn out.

When it's time to change a diaper, he's nowhere to be found.

If you're like the majority of women, you spend more time with your kids than your husband does. Not only do you take them to their baseball games and read to them at night, but you also shop for their clothes, get them to school on time, and leave work when they're sick. Regardless of what strides women have made, when it comes to raising kids, that women do more work is still the reality. What can you do about it? Probably a lot, but be prepared to go through some tension, arguments, and discomfort first.

First, let's look at how you've handled this problem so far. Are you quietly resentful? Do you make sarcastic remarks to the kids about your husband's not doing his share? Do you fly into a rage when he makes a suggestion about how to handle your son's truancy problem and blame him for it? Do you wear your weariness like a badge of suffering?

In fairness to your husband, unless you talk about the problem, he literally may not see it. He may view the fact that you spend more time with the kids as being your free choice. He feels fine about doing other things, so he assumes that if you wanted to do other things you would. You may be expecting him to read your mind and know how you feel, which isn't going to happen.

Of course, being direct and telling your husband that you want him to help more doesn't always work. A common scenario might go like this: You tell your husband that you want him to bathe the kids at night, change a diaper here and there, or give them dinner when you work late. He comes back with something like "They need a mother's love," "You change their diapers faster," or "They prefer you to feed them."

What happens then? Well, if you feel the least bit prone to guilt or believe that women *should* nurture more and care more, then these flimsy arguments will work on you.

Otherwise, if you want the work of raising the kids to be more equally divided, hold your ground. Continue to insist that your husband contribute his fair share. Be specific. Say "I want you to feed the children on Wednesday nights," "I want us to take turns putting the children to bed," or "I want you to take Brad to his soccer game every other Saturday."

Try negotiating certain responsibilities. Say, for instance, "I'll continue with the car pool if you take Johnny to Cub Scouts" or "Which would you prefer to do, the car pool or Johnny's scouts?"

If your husband complains, suggest getting in extra help: babysitters, housecleaners, a driver, whatever it takes. You can also throw in that you would prefer that he make a little less money and be home more often.

You also might want to look at your own behavior. Are you complaining yet not really wanting your husband to share the responsibility? If your identity is tied to your kids, you may have difficulty relinquishing control. Do you subvert your husband's efforts to pitch in by criticizing what he does or by saying "Oh, just let me do it." If so, it's time for you to back off and give your husband the opportunity to share in both the work and the joy of child rearing with you.

Maybe you've decided that it's not worth the fight, that you'd rather do the extra work. Living with that solution means accepting the following:

- This is your choice—in other words, you can no longer be angry at your husband for not doing his share.
- You cannot whine that your husband expects too much of you. Remember, it's you who has decided to expect this of yourself.
- You can't complain to the kids about their father.
- You cannot engage in any victim behavior in front of your friends, such as saying things like "Oh, I told Bill he might as well go to the movies without me. I have to iron the kids' clothes, fix them dinner, help them with their homework, and fix the lawnmower."

The only way to get your husband to change the behavior described in this section is for you to stand firm and to be consistent. He isn't going to make it easy for you, but if you are clear about what you want and don't get sidetracked, before long he'll come around.

I want another child, he doesn't.

If you're lucky, you and your husband agree on the number of children you want to have. Often, however, one person in a marriage wants one or more children than the other spouse. And since you either will have another child or you won't—there is no middle ground—couples often go round and round about this issue, sometimes for years without resolution. Usually the desire to have a child is so compelling that it's difficult to let go, and the wish *not* to have a child or another child is equally compelling. (Otherwise, the issue would be resolved easily.) Each partner tends to put the whole relationship onto this issue: "If you loved me, you would want to have a child with me" or "If you loved me, you wouldn't force me to have a child I don't want." Because the feelings run so deep, it's often painful and frustrating to have a rational conversation about the issue, but, of course, that's precisely what's needed. (It could just as easily be your husband who wants another child, but let's assume you do.)

Let's jump to the heart of the matter right off. If your husband continues to say no, can you accept not having a child or will you resent him later on for depriving you of having a child? If he gives in and says yes, will he later resent you for ruining his life? These are the issues that you *must* talk about openly and honestly.

You both have to be completely honest about your feelings. Disagreements about issues that come from the heart can create intense feelings of resentment, anger, and bitterness. Talk it out, *now* (not ten years from now, when it will be too late), until the two of you can come to a resolution.

Discuss with your husband what his opposition is about. Perhaps your husband says you can't afford another child: "Haven't we sacrificed our vacations to pay for the two kids we already have?" Or he thinks he doesn't get enough time with you as it is. Figure out what it is that your husband is adamant about and try to determine a way to alleviate his concerns. For instance, are you spending too much time with the kids? Have you become a mommy and ceased to be a wife? If that's the case, focus more on your marriage. Spend more time with your husband. Reassure him with your actions, not words, that you will not abandon your relationship with him if you have yet another child.

Re-evaluate your long-term goals. Was your husband counting on the income you would bring in when your last child went to kindergarten and you returned to work? Was he looking forward to some kid-free years with you?

Perhaps your husband is sick of changing diapers, going to the zoo on Super Bowl Sunday, and giving time-outs. If your husband feels overwhelmed already, pushing him for another child is not being considerate of his feelings. Ask him if this is a bad time. If you waited a year or so until Junior is out of the terrible twos, is it possible he might have a different response? What compromises are you willing to make? Can you volunteer to do most of the work of another child without complaint?

If you have been staying home with your young children, you may be fearful of entering the workplace again. Sometimes having another child to buy time is tempting. If this is the case, face those fears and insecurities head on. Becoming independent is a personal issue for you and needs to be addressed.

After talking the issue out with your husband and doing some soul-searching on your own, you may decide not to have another child. If so, you can still satisfy the urge to nurture by volunteering at a local hospital, spending some time at a preschool, or being a big sister.

But, most importantly, if you decide not to have children, you must do it without holding your husband responsible for your decision. And likewise, if your husband decides to go along with your desire to have a child, he must embrace the idea by taking responsibility for his decision.

Trouble Spot Three:

Money

Money is a practical problem for most couples. There is never enough, and most everyone has a different idea of how to spend what there is. For instance, you and your husband might disagree on whether to spend your money on a vacation or on new living room chairs. If your husband is a saver and you are a spender, then you probably argue not about what to spend money on but whether to spend it at all. Couples often consist of one saver and one spender. You may not have considered yourself a spender before you got married, but if your husband wants to spend less money than you, you are likely to be labeled the spender in the family.

How to make, spend, and save money requires a great deal of compromise because rarely do two people feel exactly the same about the subject. Say your husband likes to take chances, believing that there will always be enough money. He wants to invest in aggressive stocks and gold mines in Arizona. You on the other hand are a worrier; no matter how much money you have, you are always concerned that one day it will vanish. You prefer to invest in bonds and mutual funds. Unless you and your husband come to some compromise—such as putting some funds in safe stocks and some in Arizona gold mines—money will continue to be a source of tension or anger.

Not only is money a practical problem but a symbolic one as well. Our world may be changing, but men and women still, by and large, regard money from different standpoints. For most men money is connected to the ego, whereas most women regard money as security.

Because his ego is involved, the making and spending of money is closely connected to your husband's feelings of self-worth. Men are more likely than women to be judged by their career status—in other words, what kind of job they have and how much money they make. Even in dual-income homes, men are usually expected to be the primary provider.

Most women, on the other hand, have not been socialized to be "good providers." When a wife works, she doesn't necessarily feel the same pressure her husband does to earn the highest possible salary. More so than your husband, you may be inclined to strive for personal satisfaction as opposed to a high salary.

Because your husband has a lot riding on his ability to make money, he may interpret even the most innocent remark from you—such as "I saw Marilyn today. She's wearing a ring the size of a small mountain"—as criticism. Because he can't afford to buy you that kind of jewelry, he may react defensively. For instance, he might say Marilyn's husband is a jerk or make a general statement about how women expect men to take care of them. If he's worried about money, he may keep his concerns to himself because he thinks that talking about them with you will make him appear weak. Rather than understanding how deeply this issue affects your husband's ego, you in turn might feel angry or rejected when you come up against your husband's reluctance to talk about his feelings.

If you make more money than your husband, it's vital that you and your husband talk about finances. You may avoid the topic altogether because you're worried that your financial success will intimidate your husband, but the silence will not help. Instead it will breed resentment and misunderstandings.

Money can also be a catchall for other problems in a relationship. For instance, if you and your husband don't know how to express everyday feelings of irritation, hurt, or frustration, jabbing at each other about money might become a way to release those feelings. In my work, I find that when couples continue to fight about a particular topic without resolution, their fighting is rarely about that issue but is usually about something else. If you find yourself battling constantly with your husband about money, ask yourself if perhaps something else isn't at work. For instance, you might complain about your husband's cheapness, but what you're really upset about is his lack of affection for you. Or your disapproval of your husband's picking up the tab for dinner with his friends might hide your hurt feelings over his seeming to care more about them than about you.

Everyone's reactions to issues like religion, politics, and child rearing are based on entrenched views they learned when they were young. Money is another one of those issues. Let's say your parents taught you that going out for a nice dinner was wasteful. Your husband's family, on the other hand, loved trying every new restaurant. Unless you and your husband acknowledge the differences in the way you were raised and find some compromise, you will argue every time the subject of eating out versus eating in arises.

In this chapter are some of the most common problems I hear voiced by wives about money, along with some specific advice about how to get your husband to hear what you want to say.

He's irresponsible.

When you first met your husband, you may have been intrigued or excited by his spontaneous or generous nature. Perhaps he lavished a lot of gifts on you, insisted on picking up the tab when you went out to dinner with your folks, and impulsively suggested things like an overnight drive to Sedona to watch the sun come up there. But now there are bills to be paid, and he's still spending money on toys for himself or maybe for the kids. The behavior you once found romantic now seems irresponsible.

Often wives of such husbands find them to be alternately amusing and frustrating. One day you may be furious that your husband spent half of his paycheck on computer software, and the next day when he surprises the kids with a seven-hundred-dollar puppy, you tease him about being a "big kid."

Clearly you married a spender. If you married him convinced that you could eventually convert him into a saver, then it's you who will have to adjust your expectations. If you and your husband have separate monies and your husband chooses to spend his money on toys, let him be.

If he's spending from joint monies, then discuss your concerns with him in a calm, nonjudgmental way. If your husband is accustomed to making his own decisions, he will not take kindly to being told that you disapprove of how he is spending money. Your husband will probably feel that you are trying to fence him in and dictate what he can and cannot do. He may even interpret your disapproval as dislike. Your husband will be more open to adapting his style to fit the needs of your marriage if he feels that you love, support, and approve of him.

For some men, the idea of consulting with another person about a decision is a sign of weakness. Men are *expected* to know, *expected* to have the answers; consulting with someone else about a decision means he doesn't have the answer himself. So when you say you want to talk about money, he may say "I never discussed what I was spending with you before we got married, so why now?" When you respond, stressing the partnership is your best bet. Say "Well, being married changes things. It has nothing to do with what you're buying. It's just that my idea of marriage partners is that they talk to each other about their plans." By saying this you reframe your husband's dilemma. In a marriage it's *expected* and okay to talk about such matters. It doesn't imply that the man is weak at all.

Try to set a limit on the amount of discretionary income that your husband can spend. He may resist your effort to rein him in, but tell him that you're not doing it to get him under your control but to make *you* feel more secure. Criticizing your husband or treating him like a child won't work. Stress that your security is the issue. It's not that you want him to report in to you. Once you agree on an amount, stop talking about it and get excited when he brings home his latest toy.

If your husband is acting irresponsibly, he's spending money you don't have, and you want him to change, then changing some of your behavior will help you send a clear message to him.

- Expect him to be responsible, and talk to him as if he were. Don't be amused when he acts irresponsibly. Be consistent.
- Suggest the two of you sit down together and look over your finances. Tell him it would be helpful to you if you understood how your monies were being spent.
- If there are areas in which he's irresponsible and in which you cannot tolerate irresponsibility—paying bills for instance—say "When the bills aren't paid on time, it makes me anxious." Tell your husband that you would like to take over paying the bills to alleviate your anxiety (not to punish him).

After you begin paying the bills, there is no reason for any more discussion. In other words, you had two choices: not pay the bills and be anxious or pay the bills. You chose to pay the bills. Harping on him about his incompetence will never work. *You* have to decide what you can and cannot live with. It's also a good idea to stop commenting on irresponsible behavior that doesn't affect you. Chances are, your husband has received attention all his life for being incompetent or irresponsible. Why not be the first person in his life to notice the competent behavior and appreciate it? This is the best way to turn this behavior around.

He has a fit when I buy clothes.

As a single person, you spent your income in whatever way you chose; you decided how much money you would spend on clothes, vacations, savings, and so on. Now that you're married, your husband complains when you spend money on new clothes, a manicure, or one more pair of black boots. Moving from being single and autonomous to being married and in a partnership is difficult. It's hard finding that balance between being a separate person and being a partner in a marriage.

One of the first steps in finding that balance is to look at how your husband talks to you about your spending habits.

- Does he lecture you?
- Does he demand that you change?
- Does he berate you like a child?

If he does any of these things, you are probably not able to listen to his message because you're too busy reacting to his parental attitude. Talk to him calmly. Tell him that you would like to have a serious conversation about money but you insist that he talk to you as an equal. If he continues to fall back on old habits, call him on it immediately. Once he changes his way of communicating with you, you will be able to discuss money and come to some conclusions or compromises.

Let's say that your husband doesn't communicate in any of the ways listed, and instead he approaches you as an adult. In response to his concerns about your expenditures do you do any of the following?

- spend more just for spite and to let him know he can't boss you around
- hide your new clothes or lie about how much money you spend
- pout and feel sorry for yourself because he is depriving you of pleasure

If you respond to your husband in these ways, it's time to take a look at your behavior. By reacting in this way, you are responding to your husband as if you were a child and he were the only adult. Since marriage is a partnership, this is not a mature or helpful way to respond. It means either you're having a hard time carrying your own weight or that you have not yet shifted your priorities to suit your married situation.

Try to understand why your husband reacts the way he does. Perhaps he's worried about money or he's disappointed that you both aren't saving more towards your house or in anticipation of having a child. Maybe he's unsure about his job. Just your listening to your husband's concerns and supporting his feelings may lessen his anxiety. After you listen to his reasons for concern, he may even win you over. Either way, you will be operating as partners rather than adversaries.

If you feel that what you spend on clothes is justified and you intend to continue spending the same amount of money, tell your husband directly, like an adult.

If he's a saver and you're a spender, now that you're married he may be trying to get you to see things his way. There is definitely a need to compromise on spending issues, but you don't have to cave in to his ideas of what's appropriate. If you're convinced that your spending is within reason (compared to others in the same income bracket, for instance) hold your ground.

- Tell him what women's clothes cost.
- Take him shopping with you. By the end of the day, not only will he know how much items cost, he will probably beg you to spend more so he won't have to shop with you again.
- Ask him what spending he is willing to cut on his side.

He never buys me anything.

I rarely hear men complain that their wives never buy them anything. It's usually women who want gifts and who perceive gifts as symbols of love. Your husband may be madly in love with you, but he's also involved with his job and tennis and playing poker with the guys. As far as he's concerned, everything is just dandy at home. Now that you're married, he figures he doesn't need to buy you gifts anymore. You must know he loves you—after all, you bagged him. If your husband is neglecting you because he's distracted, then a simple, gentle reminder should do the trick. More likely, however, you've probably been bugging hubby for a token of his affection for some time, and you're getting nowhere.

Many couples go round and round about gifts. You might find yourself complaining to no avail. Your husband keeps forgetting, or simply ignoring your request, which makes you feel even more angry and rejected. Over time, asking for and not receiving a simple gift becomes the symbol for your whole relationship.

The problem is, your husband doesn't like to be told

what to do any more than you do. It makes him feel inadequate and angry. If you remind your husband over and over that he never buys you anything, he will hear this as a demand and resist you.

Independence is an important ingredient in any relationship. Even if your husband is crazy about you, he still needs to feel independent. Your nagging him to buy you something to show you how much he loves you will make him feel that he is being *forced* to care. Any natural, loving feelings he has will begin to fade, and he'll withdraw.

If you've been nagging your husband to show you how much he loves you by buying you a present, it is self-defeating for you to continue to complain. By now, even if your husband spontaneously thinks of buying you a gift, he probably won't follow through because it would make him feel that he is caving in. He's probably decided to wait until you haven't mentioned it for a while, so it can truly be his idea, but chances are you never wait long enough! This kind of standoff can go on forever!

You can't force your husband to be generous, but you can make giving to you seem like an attractive proposition. The following are some suggestions you might try:

- Stop demanding gifts from him and complaining that he never buys you anything.
- Tell him how much it means to you when he does something for you—no matter how small or seemingly self-serving.
- Look for other ways in which your husband is giving to you and comment on them positively. Say "Thanks for listening to me last night. That was a real gift, and it helped a lot."

Say you remind your husband twenty-five times that he

never buys you anything. One day he does, and you find you have mixed feelings. You're happy he finally bought you something but then you get your knickers in a twist because you're sure he did it only to make you happy—or worse because you nagged him. You husband picks up on your ambivalence right away and feels like he can't win.

Perhaps there's some truth to your husband's feeling that he can't win. If you find yourself complaining and then discounting the efforts your husband makes, it's a good idea to look at your own behavior. Are you routinely disappointed? Do you manage to find something wrong with your husband's attempts at pleasing you? For instance, the gift isn't quite what you wanted, candles on the table isn't what you meant when you said you wanted a romantic evening, and if your husband really wanted to please *you* he would have suggested Paris rather than the Bahamas for a vacation.

If this is the case, perhaps your expectations are simply too high. Thinking that your husband never quite measures up is a way to maintain distance and avoid intimacy. Make a concerted effort to validate your husband's efforts. You could even take the first step and surprise your husband with a gift! After all, there's no better way to teach than by example.

He makes financial decisions without me because he still sees me as the naive young woman he married.

When you got married, having someone take care of you may have made you feel safe and loved. But now, you've hit your stride on the job or you're involved in your community or the children's schools. You've matured and gained a lot of confidence; perhaps you've made some more friends. You feel stymied, however, when you try to assert this newfound independence and maturity in your marriage. The problem, as you see it, is that your husband hasn't changed with you; he still sees you as a naive young woman.

Although you want your relationship to shift, you may, out of habit or anxiety, be giving your husband conflicting messages. For example, when your husband talks about your life insurance, bank accounts, stocks, and so on, do you show your disinterest by not giving him your full attention or by changing the subject? Do you say things similar to the following?

- Oh, why don't you handle it, honey? I don't understand how to do it.
- I'm so glad I have you to deal with all that stuff.
- You know I hate to call the bank.

If these comments sound familiar yet you're bothered by your husband's treatment of you, then you're giving your husband a mixed message. If you want to stop being treated like a girl, it's important that you act like a woman. Some women believe that if they can do things for themselves, men will find them aggressive. They fear their husbands won't feel needed or strong and will find another (helpless) woman to love. I would suggest that you give your husband more credit than that. The more you feel in charge of your life, the less you will feel dependent on your husband. Although your husband may be conflicted in some ways about your independence, in the long run, it is the healthiest way to go in a relationship.

If your husband still sees you as a girl, try changing your behavior.

- Don't put your husband into a parental role by constantly asking for his advice or permission on subjects you can take care of yourself.
- Learn about your investments. Ask specific questions. Take notes so you won't ask the same question over and over.
- Form your own opinions about the kinds of investments you prefer. For instance, do you like risky or safe investments?

Your husband may resist your new behavior or say things like

- Let me handle it.
- I don't have time to teach you. It's easier for me just to do it.
- It's too complicated.
- I'll take care of you.
- I'm doing a good job. Why rock the boat?

Be kind but firm about wanting to know what's going on with your finances. Say "I know you have our best interests at heart, but we're a team. I think it's good to share responsibilities and knowledge." Don't take no for an answer.

If your husband insists on maintaining control, tell him that that is unacceptable to you. Say "I'm sorry if this is difficult for you, but this is my future as well. Although I don't like to think about it, something might happen to you, and if it did I'm sure you wouldn't want me to be floundering around and at the mercy of other people. I need to understand our finances."

Keep at it and be consistent. Don't fall back into a dependent pattern if you are anxious. Just say "I'm anxious about our IBM stock" or "These interest rates are killing our savings" without implying that your husband should do something about it. Eventually your husband will come around, and someday he may even come to appreciate sharing his feelings about finances with you.

I make more money than he does, which seems to upset him.

Many women who make more money than their husbands say quickly—too quickly—that the situation is entirely comfortable for them. Sometimes this is a defensive response. Perhaps their friends are skeptical and put pressure on them to fess up that it's tough to switch roles. Women often still feel "entitled" to be taken care of. When this doesn't happen, some resentment is likely to surface, even if they think they're liberated. Even couples who have gone beyond prescribed gender roles and are 100 percent comfortable with their situations can't help but be aware of the prejudices others have.

Before we talk about handling your husband's response to this issue, let's make sure that you aren't sending your husband a mixed message.

When your husband talks about his job, do you do any of the following?

- make wistful comments about being unable to go to Hawaii again this year
- get impatient
- tell him what to do

- say "Well, I wouldn't let my boss push me around like that!"

If any of this sounds familiar, *you* may be harboring resentment about your situation. In that case, you're probably giving your husband the impression (words to the contrary) you don't respect him.

It's important that you re-evaluate your goals and feelings. To get back on track with what's really important, remember that marriage is a partnership—that means both partners are willing to do what's necessary to make the partnership work. Look again at your husband and remind yourself of the qualities that you married him for. If you are unhappy with your work, then discuss with him the possibility of changing jobs. If you enjoy your job, appreciate that you are being paid well to do it.

Also, talk to your husband about your feelings. Many women who make more money than their husbands put aside their own feelings for fear that expressing them will hurt their husbands' already bruised egos. Your feelings are important too; assume your husband can handle them. If you think that your husband doesn't appreciate your efforts, say so. If you had a positive experience with the president of the company, tell your husband about it. Don't fall into hiding your enthusiasm. It will only lead to resentment.

Let's say you're comfortable with your situation and your husband is having a hard time. Although times are definitely changing, it's still generally assumed that men will make more money than their wives. Your husband may be feeling shaky and embarrassed about your topsy-turvy situation. After all he's not living up to his view of what is expected of men. His discomfort can come out in many ways. Even if you talk about it and he tells you he's fine with it, he may still harbor some resentment or feelings of inadequacy. Does your husband do any of the following?

- make disparaging jokes about you "wearing the pants" in the family
- seem defeated
- refuse to talk about money
- find ways to criticize you
- act embarrassed around his friends when they talk about money

Perhaps his discomfort comes out when you discuss such things as vacations, buying clothes, or going out to dinner with friends. Your husband may become tense or avoid discussions about such things because he doesn't feel comfortable about spending "your" money. It's essential that you and your husband discuss the issue; avoiding the topic will only make it worse. On the other hand, don't push your husband to reveal his intimate, fragile feelings if he resists. Just discussing the mechanics of the problem will do, there's no need for your husband to feel even more vulnerable or one down by having to dredge up feelings of inadequacy.

Following are some suggestions about how to become a team:

- Make it clear that you have a partnership.
- Ask your husband his thoughts about vacations.
- Comment on situations that are uncomfortable instead of pretending they didn't happen. For instance, say "Brad was a real jerk for asking whether I paid for your new car."

50

He's worried about his job, but I can't get him to talk about it.

While you may be willing to talk about the painful aspects of your life, your husband may be unwilling. It doesn't come naturally to most men to express their worries or concerns. Many prefer to draw away from others and try to figure out a solution on their own. Talking about a problem often makes a man feel worse.

Assume that your husband will talk about his job eventually, once he's had a chance to mull over his situation alone. Don't get impatient and expect him to act as you would in the same circumstance. When you pressure him to talk before he's ready, it leads to more withdrawal, anger, and resentment. Instead, try the following strategies:

- Give your husband the space he needs. Stop asking questions and demanding that he talk to you about his job.
- Don't assume that because your husband isn't talking to you about his job concerns that he isn't dealing with the problem. In most cases, he is indeed confronting the problem, but in his own way.

- Talk about your worries with some close women friends. This way, you can satisfy your need to express your feelings about how your husband's work problem is affecting you yet give your husband the time he needs to explore the problem in his fashion without pressure from you.

In the meantime
- Don't make sarcastic remarks about finances.
- Don't pick a fight about something else and then throw in comments about his job.
- Don't let your anxiety spill out constantly. Try to contain it, or talk with someone else.
- Go about your business of taking care of the kids, doing your own work, and visiting with friends.

When your husband emerges from his seclusion and tells you some plan he's hatched up to relieve his job stress, don't punish him for being gone by withdrawing from him. By accepting that he has a different way of confronting problems, you show him respect and give him support.

If as time goes by the situation worsens and you think your husband may lose his job or you feel that he's seriously depressed, say "I'm worried about our situation. I know it's difficult, but I'd like us to spend some time talking about our feelings and our options. If now is not a good time, when is?"

Be empathic but firm. Stress that you are a team and need to work on the problem together. Get practical. Say "I know talking is hard, but it's time for you to talk to someone. What about Fred? He went through a job change last year. Or how about a professional job counselor?"

If he still refuses to talk, then tell him you need answers to some major questions, like How much money do you have? How long will it last? and How can you tighten your belts even more? You need him to discuss these questions. Don't take no for an answer. When your husband realizes that you are supportive and that you need information, not necessarily an outpouring of feelings, he will be more able to respond to you. The feelings may follow.

Trouble Spot Four:

Sex

Men are rarely complicated when it comes to sex. Women on the other hand are extremely so. Men definitely have their anxieties, but they focus more on scoring and performance. Women, in contrast, get their emotions connected to the sexual act. You are much more likely than your husband to imbue sex with overtones of love, romance, and acceptance.

No matter what mood the two of you are in—even if you're angry with or distant to one another—your husband may still express an interest in sex. When you were dating you may have found this particular behavior romantic, thinking it meant he couldn't get enough of you. Now you may feel it doesn't have anything to do with you. "He only wants sex" is a comment I hear from a lot of women. Many wives find this odd or even distasteful, but for your husband, it's perfectly natural. Although your husband probably agrees with you about what romance is, he doesn't need to have romance as part of his sexuality. In fact, many men like to have sex at least some of the time without any hint of romance at all. That's when they hint about those high heels and leather teddies. Their wives, on the other hand, have sex as much for the hugs, kisses, and cuddling as for the actual sexual act. This may be a biological difference, but it's hard to keep that in mind when you're feeling misunderstood and your husband is feeling rejected. If you each view sex only from your perspective, you're both likely to feel confused, hurt, and angry.

When you say no to sex, it may be because of a variety of reasons—you have morning sickness, you're tired, you're angry, you're not in the mood. Those are all totally valid reasons, but for many women saying no is uncomfortable. Some women have a hard time honoring their own feelings, so saying no translates into depriving their spouse. You might say yes because you feel you should, because you don't want to hurt your husband's feelings, or because you worry that your husband will leave you if you don't perform. Or, if you're shy or have low sexual self-esteem, you may be uncomfortable asking your husband to satisfy your sexual desires as well as his own. Your husband might find your behavior confusing. He may feel dissatisfied with the sex himself, sensing that you're doing it for him, and he may not know how to go about pleasing you. Or he might not involve himself in your psychology at all and simply take your sheepish "OK" for a gung-ho "Yes!" There's also the chance that he feeds your insecurity by implying that you should be a willing partner whenever he's in the mood.

No one wants to feel thwarted or rejected in any area, but this is especially true about sex. Having sex is an act of vulnerability. You are literally (usually) naked with someone, and naked emotionally as well, open to being deeply wounded. Both you and your husband can be hurt if you don't have an understanding about saying no. If you were accustomed to doing it like bunnies when you were first together, you have to adjust to the fact that no two people want to have sex at the same time all the time. This issue needs to be discussed with sensitivity. Unfortunately, earlier in your relationship you may have resolved arguments by having passionate sex, but now sex is more likely to cause an argument.

You may argue because there's never enough time. Perhaps he wants a quickie before work, but you're still smarting from your argument the night before. Or he wants to do it at the most inopportune time—five minutes before your kids are due home from school. When you say no, he complains that you're not the same woman he married. You shoot back that he doesn't buy you flowers anymore and besides he just thinks of himself when it comes to sex, so why bother?

If you find yourself saying no a lot, you may be avoiding sex out of anger, disappointment, or resentment about other marital issues. Sex is a powerful weapon to use in a relationship, and sometimes it's just too tempting for one party or the other to withhold it as a way of expressing anger. If you're very busy it's also tempting to give sex a backseat to work, kids, or vacuuming the rug, but it's not wise. In order to stay close to your husband and have a *marital* rather than a *platonic* relationship, you have to communicate about sex and work to keep your sex life interesting and active.

If you and your husband develop a sexual problem— many of you will during the course of your marriage—it's essential that you talk about it. You may feel as if you have to walk on eggs to protect his fragile ego, but so be it. It's true that men are sensitive about their sexuality, but so are you. Men, of course, are more vulnerable. They can't hide it if they're having a performance problem the way women often can—although a sensitive man will pick it up right away if you're faking it. If you feel too embarrassed to talk about your own feelings about a problem *you're* having or if you don't acknowledge a problem your husband is experiencing, I can guarantee you the problem will only get worse. Either your sexual performance or your husband's will suffer, and one or both of you will begin to withdraw.

I know talking about sex won't be easy. Most people in our culture have not learned how to talk about sex with the opposite sex. Perhaps you can talk with a woman friend about your sexual problems more easily than you can share them with your husband. And your husband might know how to do "guy talk" about sex but doesn't have a clue about how to talk about sex with his wife. But that's what this book is all about: helping you and your husband to talk to each other about the issues that are important. Once you both get started it will become easier over time.

In this chapter you'll read what wives find most difficult to talk to their spouses about when it comes to sex, along with some suggestions about how to go about discussing these issues with your husband.

He wants to do it all the time.

Is your husband asking all the time because you're saying no all the time? Maybe by now you're expecting him to "demand" sex, and you're automatically saying no when he asks. It's time to examine your own behavior to see what messages you're giving your husband. If you're withholding sexually because you're angry that your husband doesn't pay enough attention to you, looks at other women all the time, or doesn't take out the garbage like he's supposed to, it's your responsibility to break the ice and talk to your husband about what's going on.

If you don't feel you're guilty of holding out and not telling your husband why, the next step is to examine your husband's behavior. Is he following you around the house pinching your fanny, blowing in your ear, and jumping out at you from behind the shower door? Would he do it five times a day if you agreed to? If this is the case, give your husband a ball park figure on how much sex is comfortable for you. If you're constantly in the position of saying no, your husband may resent you and complain that you're in control of his sexual impulses or that you're withholding pleasure from him. You're much better off saying "I like to have sex about twice a week. I'm willing to have sex a bit more than that, but not three times a day." This way your husband has a clear picture and doesn't have to keep asking. If he does keep asking, you can repeat what you already told him. This is a good way to stop feeling guilty for saying no.

Perhaps it's not that your husband wants to do it all the time, but that he wants to do it at the *wrong* time for you. Help him out: tell him when *you* like to have sex. Early in the morning? Late at night? Also tell him when you don't like to have sex. When the kids are due home any minute? When you're exhausted? When you're on the phone with your mother?

Then, don't leave it to your husband to pick the right time for you; approach him when you feel like it. If your husband has completely taken over on the sexual front, you probably don't know when you want sex because you've been so busy fending him off. Tell him to give you some breathing room and why he should. Be honest. Only then can you begin to pay attention to your own signals about sex.

Be prepared to wait out a dry spell while you tune in to your own sexual rhythm. If necessary, make it clear to your husband that you need to have equal control for a while, or even full control, of when you have sex. This will be difficult for him, but it's essential if the two of you want to get back on track sexually.

If you try all of the above and your husband still doesn't take no for an answer, check how clear you've been. Are you sending him double messages? If you're unclear about sex, perhaps you're saying no so sheepishly that your husband is construing it to be yes. If you give in when you don't want sex and after you've said no a few times and then feel guilty, your husband may feel confused about your message. You may actually be training him to ask repeatedly because he knows you always say yes after two nos!

It's not romantic enough for me.

Earlier in your relationship, your husband may have told you how beautiful you were and how he wanted to make love to you fifteen different ways. Perhaps he sprinkled rose petals on the bed, offered you champagne, and even wrote you a poem or two. Or perhaps he took you to a romantic restaurant and for a walk on the beach before getting down to making love—next to the fireplace, of course. Now he grabs your bum or boob, squeezes it, and says "Let's do it." Maybe he doesn't even say "let's do it," but simply rolls over to your side of the bed in the morning and starts up.

If your husband feels a sexual impulse, he's apt to act on it. Sex, bare bones, no frills, is often just hunky-dory with him. He may feel that you are uptight if you keep saying no or if you get insulted. He thinks you have a problem. In fact, instead of understanding what you find lacking about your sex, he may feel angry that you are withholding from him or feel that you're trying to control him by forcing him to make every sexual encounter romantic.

Perhaps quickies here and there are fine with you if it's balanced by romance at other times. Tell your husband just that. In this way, you acknowledge his feelings and yours at the same time. Most men like romance too, but now that the "courting" stage is over, being romantic may not occur to your husband quite so often. As long as he doesn't feel that you're being demanding, he will probably be open to having romantic sex with you.

No one likes to feel that they are being controlled, your husband included, so now is a good time to assess your own motivation. Are you being demanding of your husband? Are you putting up your own roadblocks for closeness? Many women who are uncomfortable about sex roll out the "It's not romantic enough for me" rationale to keep a husband at bay.

Assuming you're sincere about wanting more romance

and welcoming it, I recommend you give your husband some help. It doesn't matter if he bought you flowers ten years ago and should know that's what you like. Tell your husband *exactly* what you want—flowers, an hour of conversation, some strawberries balanced on your navel. Don't expect him to think of everything.

If your husband makes the effort to create romance— let's say he gets the strawberries right—but it's still not what you expected, give the guy a break. The old saying about attracting more flies with honey than with vinegar is definitely apt here. Focus on his attempt; he will thrive on the positive reinforcement and gradually do more of what you like on his own. If you criticize his attempts and he begins to feel like what he's doing is never good enough, that there's always a "Yes, but . . . ," he will stop trying to please you altogether.

You don't have to leave it to your husband to make sex romantic. You can take the initiative, too. Ask him what *he* thinks is romantic. Then, involve him in a plan for a romantic evening or afternoon. Planning it can be exciting too. Tell your husband your romantic fantasies; don't make him guess what they are. So what if you're shy? You may be expecting your husband to go out of his way to do things that make him shy too. Fair is fair. Your husband will probably be very excited and willing to help you experience your fantasies if you share them with him.

Sometimes losing the romance in a relationship boils down to pure laziness on the part of both parties. Maybe you take each other for granted. Maybe neither of you make an effort anymore to please each other or make special time for each other. If this is the case, your sex life can become boring. Take the initiative and surprise him with a romantic picnic at a secluded beach, a night at a fancy hotel, or a simple arm-in-arm walk around your neighborhood instead of turning on the tube.

If you've tried to make the sex romantic and your husband doesn't get the point, he may be resisting you for other reasons. If you complain a lot about the lack of romance in your relationship, he may be at the point where "giving in" to you will mean losing face for him.

Everyone is vulnerable sexually. If you have made him feel inadequate instead of making him feel like a co-conspirator, he may have trouble performing, or he may withhold sex from you out of anger. Let him take control again. If you haven't been having sex at all, then going back to the kind of sex he's comfortable with for a while may be necessary to help him get his confidence back.

We have to make an appointment to have sex.

In the old days you could have sex anywhere, anytime, and perhaps you did. You didn't have to worry about the kids barging in while you were finding a new way to use the kitchen table, the living room rug, or the loungers in the backyard.

Now with kids and jobs and all your other obligations, you and your husband rarely find the time to be spontaneous. Instead, as you're cooking dinner your husband says "How about tonight after the kids are asleep and the Knicks game is over?" If his overture makes you feel that you and the Knicks were in a competition and you just lost, you're not likely to be overwhelmed with lust. You might say "I have to give myself a manicure. How about after my nails dry?" Rather than hearing your sarcasm, however, your husband might well respond with an OK. This is not to say that your husband doesn't miss the old days as well, but he may be more comfortable catching as catch can. He may not be feeling as though something is missing as much as you are.

Talk to your husband about your feelings, not in an angry, accusatory way but as a partner. "Gosh, I feel like we have to have an appointment to have sex. I miss the old days." Give him an opening to discuss how he feels about it, and maybe the two of you can make an effort to have some spontaneous sex once again. Chances are if your husband knows you're missing him sexually, he'll rise to the occasion.

If you really try, you can still find the time to check out that new sofa in the living room (just make sure the kids are in school). Instead of seeing it as making an appointment, why not see it as sharing a secret? When you both know something fun and exciting is going to happen in a few hours, it's a great way to be close and loving.

Of course, having to make an appointment for sex may not be what's really bothering you. Do you feel that other things are missing in your relationship, such as romance or connection in general? To be more precise, do you feel as if your husband doesn't have time for you anymore or that he would prefer to be doing other things? Are you resentful about how little time you have for yourself, let alone for your sex life? Have you and your husband lost touch with each other?

Your husband may not have a clue that these things are troubling you. Because you haven't brought it to his attention, he thinks everything is fine. If you're expecting him to tune in to the subtleties of your feelings, save yourself some time and hurt feelings and just tell him what's going on. Be specific and direct. Say

- I want you to be more attentive to me.
- Let's go out to dinner Friday night, just you and me.
- I miss you.

Don't say

- You don't have time for me anymore.
- I suppose if I looked like Madonna you would find more time to be with me.
- You don't care about my feelings.

Perhaps you're as guilty as your husband of neglecting the sexual side of your marriage. Try pouncing on your husband when he comes out of the shower, or better yet climb in the shower with him.

He doesn't please me.

Do you feel as if your husband should know exactly what to do to please you sexually? Have you ever uttered a word about what turns you on or given any indication that what you were getting wasn't what you wanted? If not, do you blame your husband for your lack of pleasure all the same? Men rarely make women responsible for their pleasure, and they don't expect you to guess either. They know what they like and usually set about trying to get it. Women, however, often lay the burden for figuring out their sexual pleasure on their mates. If, like some women, you submerged your own sexual needs in the beginning of your relationship out of a desire to please your guy, your husband will be even more confused. Not only does he not know what you want, but he's operating under the myth that everything you're doing for *him* is turning *you* on.

If you're shy about sex, you may find yourself blaming your husband for not getting your needs met. But you can't expect your husband, no matter how much experience he's had, to know how to take care of your sexual needs without your helping him with a clue or two. Take responsibility for your own pleasure. Tell your husband what you like and ask him to do it, or do it yourself if you can. If he doesn't get it, show him. When he hits the jackpot, let him know!

If your husband has tried to do what you like in the past and you've been critical, he might be reluctant to try again. It may be that your husband doesn't like to do what you like. Just as your husband shouldn't force you to do something you don't want to do, you can't force your husband to like a certain sexual act.

If you've told your husband what you like, yet he still insists on doing it his way, then say it again. In the meantime, let's consider some reasons why he might not be willing to do what it is you want. Is he shy? Is he afraid of doing it wrong? Some men insist on having sex their way because they are nervous about performance or about looking foolish, just as you are.

Then again, some people, men and women alike, are sexually selfish. If your husband doesn't please you because he's into pleasing himself, tell him that game is over. If you must, stop doing what is pleasuring strictly for him until he reciprocates. Give him a lot of positive feedback when he makes you feel good, and eventually he will get pleasure from that as well.

He likes it dirty, I like it clean.

Let's say after three strenuous, sweaty sets of tennis, you come home, throw off your clothes, and head for the shower. On the way, your husband pounces on you and insists that he's got to have you *now*. Or, worse yet, maybe he comes home from his tennis game dripping sweat and starts rubbing up against your clean body.

Both men and women are sensitive to smells, but they seem to be sensitive to different varieties of them! What turns your husband on—your sweaty body or his sweaty body next to yours—may do nothing for you. However, if you suggest your Tarzan take a shower, he gets miffed. "Where's the spontaneity?," he might thunder, or "What's the big deal about a little sweat?" or even "I love the way you smell."

How do you say in the kindest fashion that his sweat doesn't turn you on? Just say it. You can even tell your husband it's your problem, which it is. There is no right or wrong about this issue, it's just a question of preference. If you're turned off by sweat or smells, be up front about it. Better to say how you feel than to go ahead and have sex but not enjoy it.

A pleasant way around this dilemma is to suggest that you and your husband take a shower together. Even if he sees through this ruse, he probably won't complain because taking showers together is fun.

Reaction to smells is visceral, and we're stuck with our reactions. But there are other preferences that both you and your husband have that perhaps you could be more open to experimenting with or compromising on. For instance, perhaps you like to do it in the dark, while your husband likes it in broad daylight, with the windows open and while Mr. Smith is trimming his hedge next door.

Maybe you like to do it in the dark because you're shy or because you don't like your body. Talk to your husband—yes, you can—and tell him you would like to be more experimental, but you need his support. Go slow. Start with sex in the morning with the shades down. Work up to sex when Mr. Smith is in his front yard. If at any time you get uncomfortable, tell your husband and stop what you're doing or, in this case, wait until dark.

Remember that sex is about fun, closeness, and intimacy. You should never be in the position of doing something you don't want to do. If your husband has a specific fantasy and you can't get into it, he'll be disappointed, but most people are flexible when it comes to sex. You can probably find something else for the two of you to do that you both enjoy.

The most important message here is that sex is for your joint enjoyment. Sometimes spouses will do certain things that they're not crazy about because they know it drives their mates crazy. If you can do that, great. If not, don't worry about it. However, if you do feel that you're more uptight about sex than you really want to be, tell your husband, but make it clear that whatever experimentation you do has to be in a safe, comfortable, and supportive environment.

I'm afraid to talk about our sexual problem because it might hurt his feelings.

Chances are, if you're worried about your husband's fragile ego, it's probably dovetailing with your own shyness about talking about sex. Not talking about a problem will eventually make it worse. If your husband doesn't get an erection or ejaculates prematurely once or twice, this does *not* constitute a problem. Talking about it may make him even more uncomfortable. Use your sensitivity and good judgment. If it happens a few more times, ask him what's going on. (It's always a good idea to be checked out by a doctor if sudden sexual problems occur. Many medications and the onset of some medical conditions are frequently the cause of sexual problems.)

If the problem continues and you decide to talk to your husband, don't say

- You didn't get it up again.
- You never had this problem before.
- You don't find me sexually attractive anymore.

Instead, ask an open-ended question: "What's happening?" Let your husband tell you what's going on. Don't put words in his mouth. If he leaves it vague—he's anxious about work, he has a lot on his mind—let it be. Tell him that if there is anything you can do he should let you know.

Don't take on your husband's problem. If you get emotionally involved in whether your husband gets an erection and take it as a personal failure when he doesn't, then he will feel double pressure, both from himself and you.

Don't get angry, either, or sulk and act hurt. This will only aggravate the situation. Instead, go on about the business of being sexually satisfied yourself. There are plenty of ways for you to get sexual satisfaction with your husband without having intercourse, as I'm sure you know.

If you are still being sexually satisfied or are allowing him to sexually satisfy you in other ways, your husband has one less thing to feel guilty, worried, or upset about.

If the problem continues, then approach him again and tell him you're concerned. You can say that you think it may be something other than sex that's bothering him and you'd like to know what it is and if you can help.

If you're having a problem, for instance, with relaxing, lubricating, or orgasm, take a deep breath and talk to your husband about what's going on. Only when he knows what's wrong can he help you. You can also talk to a close woman friend; sometimes running your fears or confusion by another woman can be helpful. Many women for instance are not prepared for the changes that happen as they begin to move toward menopause: vaginal dryness, a change in response times, fluctuations of sexual interest. Talking to someone else or reading a few books can be reassuring and will help you to talk to your husband about what's going on.

Don't shift the blame for whatever problem you're having to your husband and attack his sexual performance. If you are withdrawing from your husband sexually, examine why. Often it's not a sexual issue, but something outside of the sexual relationship. If it is in the sexual arena, figure out what's bothering you. Is he inattentive? Are you feeling unattractive, old, uninteresting? Are you afraid he's losing interest and so withdrawing from him out of defense?

Women especially can go through periods of not liking their bodies or feeling sexually unattractive. It's not fair to cut off your husband because you're feeling bad about yourself. He won't understand what's going on and will feel hurt, rejected, or angry, none of which will help with your self-image. Ask your husband to help you with this problem. Tell him you need extra attention. If it's your husband who is going through difficulty, give him the same support you would like to have.

Trouble Spot Five:
Daily Life

Let's face it—simply living together on a daily basis can be a challenge. You're an early riser; your husband loves sleeping in. You like to ski; your husband prefers golf. You enjoy quiet meals at home with friends; your husband wants to meet them in a noisy, crowded restaurant. Resolving all these differences—in any given day there are dozens of them—requires compromise.

Perhaps, in the beginning of your relationship, you and your husband reveled in your differences and each appreciated the other's sense of humor. You listened to each other with respect and answered thoughtfully. You laughed at each other's jokes and observations. Now, after a few years, you don't talk, you argue. You wave him off saying "I don't want to hear another lecture on China," and he cuts you off mid-sentence with "That's a typical liberal response." Maybe you've heard the same joke so many times you could scream, and he says your comments about his family are no longer funny, they're caustic.

After a few years of marriage, perhaps you've noticed that your husband is focused on his *own* goals, whereas there's a good chance that you've made your *husband* your project. More women than men are seized with the compulsion to change their spouse's behavior. The manners issue is a good example. Many men comfortably burp, talk with their mouths full, or even spit in public, while women rarely do. Why this occurs is a mystery, since we're all raised by the same parents. Regardless, when your husband does these things in your company you probably feel embarrassed and then obligated to correct him. You quickly find, however, that just telling him he eats with his mouth open doesn't change his behavior. Trying to embarrass him doesn't work. Nagging him about it doesn't change him, either, but you keep doing it anyway. Now on the ride home after every evening out, you catalog his offenses: he told a stupid joke with his mouth full, he wasn't sensitive to one of the guests, he spoke rudely, he ignored the waiter.

This kind of behavior reaches its peak when your husband eats, drinks, or smokes too much, and you think it's your duty to hound him into changing these behaviors *for his own good.* But, again, instead of appreciating your concern and attempts to educate him, he feels controlled and resents your interference. You've been trained to focus on the needs and well-being of others, so this will be difficult for you to change, but it's important that you do so.

Often, men and women handle everyday grievances in very different ways. It's a good idea to explore how you cope with everyday problems, disagreements, and annoyances. Women tend to have difficulty expressing anger directly. Your husband is probably better at it. If you don't like something, instead of saying so, you might just grin and bear it (and resent it) or complain so subtly that your husband doesn't get it. Or, when your husband expresses his angry feelings directly, instead of appreciating his candor, you end up feeling hurt and abused.

Most people also drift back and forth from closeness to separateness. You and your husband both have a different rhythm: when you feel connected he doesn't or vice versa. It can be painful, confusing, and angering. And, because you're so close, you see the best and the worst of each other. If you're in a bad mood, you may hide it from others and take it out on your husband. Minor disagreements can build to major conflicts. Your unresolved differences can lead to a home filled with tension.

It's often difficult to keep the big picture of your commitment and love for each other in mind from day to day. It's too easy to get bogged down arguing about the same irritants over and over. Learning to approach your husband in a different way and working on change together is a more efficient way of working out everyday problems.

Your relationship may be suffering in other areas. For instance, if you're not talking productively about money or sex, your frustration may surface in everyday complaints about how your husband brushes his teeth, never puts gas in the car, or insists on closing every phone call with "Ciao." Getting bogged down in these kinds of complaints makes talking about the big issues impossible. You and your husband can remain angry and distant with each other for days, weeks, or months without ever managing to say what's really bothering you. For many couples, it boils down to never learning how to have a "good fight."

Of course, there is behavior that you absolutely don't

have to accept. For instance, if your husband is critical of you, makes sarcastic remarks, or refuses to do his share of the housework. On the other hand, what he eats, how he eats, and when he eats might be behavior you would be better off forcing yourself not to comment on, even though it's annoying or upsetting to you. Learning to distinguish when it's a good idea to talk about what's bugging you and when it's better to leave your husband to his own habits is a useful tool.

He makes plans without consulting me.

You probably wouldn't say yes to a social engagement without discussing it with your husband first. Chances are you even consult your husband about separate plans you make with a friend for dinner or tennis. To you, this is not asking permission, you are simply being considerate of your partner. Your husband, on the other hand, may call you at the last minute to tell you he's made dinner plans for both of you with some friends or business associates. Or it doesn't occur to him to tell you if he's made plans to play racquetball with a friend or even that he's planning on watching basketball right after dinner. If you bring this up to your husband, however, he might get angry and say something like "Do you want me to ask your permission?"

Your husband's taking charge has probably been reinforced all his life. As he sees it, you are now asking him to do just the opposite. Instead of taking charge, he's supposed to ask your permission—something he considers demeaning and something he thinks others will see as demeaning as well.

Talk with your husband. Acknowledge his different

perspective but stress the partnership aspect of your marriage. Tell him that for you it has nothing to do with reporting in or asking permission. You're not trying to curb his independence, but simply to live together in a respectful way, which to you means sharing in decision making.

Say "I would like you to tell me when you've made some 'tentative' plans for us to get together with friends and ask me what I think. Or at least inform me ahead of time if you're planning on going to play golf with Fred or to watch a basketball game. This is not to control you, it's so I can feel included."

Often this is all it takes to get your husband to understand your feelings and to accommodate you. Once he realizes what you want and why, you make it easy for him to change his behavior. He may forget a few times, so remind him if he does. Eventually he will come around.

If you've been telling your husband for years to inform you about plans but he doesn't change, maybe he feels controlled by you. If you don't take the time to explain why it's important that he consult you but simply show him your anger, he may not understand what the issue is. He may see it strictly as another way that you're trying to undermine his independence. No one likes to feel forced to adhere to someone else's demands.

If you have tried everything, including explaining your feelings, and he still doesn't get it, tell him that the next time he makes plans without discussing them with you, you won't go. Then, no matter what, follow through. This may seem drastic, but it's the only way you're going to get his attention. If he is accustomed to doing things his way and not adjusting to the different expectations of a partnership, then it's time to show him, instead of telling

74

him, that there are consequences to his behavior.

The first time you say no, he may insist that you go anyway, saying things like "You aren't serious, are you?" or "Come on, you're getting carried away" or "Okay, you made your point, now come on."

Stick to your guns. If he continues to push, say "I told you that I would not go the next time." Don't say it with anger, but matter-of-factly. This is important—you don't want to give your husband any ammunition to turn the issue into your doing something wrong. Stay focused on his behavior and make it clear that what you are doing is a consequence of *his* behavior. He will change his behavior.

I do most of the work.

It's hard to negotiate the balance of power in a relationship. Your husband may feel entitled—because he makes more money than you, because he's a man, because he says he needs more sleep than you—to being taken care of at home and released from the drudgery of household work. But there is no reason why you have to fall for the idea that housework is your job, although many women do.

Each partner in a relationship has equal rights to personal time. If you are working the same amount of hours as your husband, that entitles you to the same amount of free time. If your husband is the kind of guy who feels entitled to be taken care of, now is a good time to see if you're reinforcing those very notions that you say you want him to change.

When he leaves his clothes strewn around and his coffee cup on the table, expecting them to magically disappear, do you do any of the following?

- get angry but decide it's not worth the hassle, and just do whatever needs to be done
- sometimes pick up after him and other times blow a gasket
- entertain his friends with jokes about how incapable your husband is

If you're doing any of these things, chances are your husband isn't going to change. In fact, you are training him not to take your complaints and requests for change seriously.

If you feel like a second-class citizen in your marriage because you're afraid to "rock the boat," then nothing will change other than the level of your resentment, which will continue to rise. If you want change, don't leave it to your husband to raise the issue. You will have to speak up. Say "I work as much as you do, but I end up doing more at home, which isn't fair. We need to share more of the chores."

Here are some suggestions to help you to elicit your husband's cooperation:

- Ask your husband directly for help. Don't expect him to volunteer, and don't expect him to pick up on your subtle hints.
- Show him what to do, and if need be tell him how to do it. Rolling your eyes when he tells you he's never run a vacuum cleaner and then leaving him on his own is not helpful. Show him how to vacuum a rug. (Laugh about it later, when you're in the shower.)
- Divvy up the chores. Make sure there are consequences for your husband's not doing what's on his list of chores. If he forgets to pick up the clothes at the cleaners and

consequently has no ironed shirts, don't volunteer to iron a shirt for him. Let him figure out a solution himself, and meanwhile don't give him a hard time about it. It's his problem. Let him take care of it in his own way.

- Try doing things together. Have a cleaning day once a week or once a month, during which you work side by side.
- Don't redo work your husband has done or complain about his shoddy work. If it's his job to wash the windows and dust, bite your tongue and don't comment if it's not up to your standards. If you do criticize, he will resent you and stop cooperating. All of this will be particularly difficult if your husband, on top of not doing his share, is also a slob. If you redo his work, he probably won't notice or care.

The following are a few of the comments I've heard from husbands along with some suggested responses for you.

- If your husband says "I make more money than you do," tell him that you work as many hours, and the amount of money shouldn't be the issue. You can also remind him that women across the country make sixty-nine cents to every dollar that men make.
- He might try "My job is more demanding." But don't fall for the argument that because your husband is a man he's under more pressure than you on the job. Don't argue about details, simply say "I disagree." However, if your husband is working twice the hours you are and making more money for *both of you*, then you should be willing to adjust your demands as well.
- If he says "You can cook a meal a lot faster than I can," you can first have a chuckle about this one. And then say "I trust you. You can learn."

If you've tried everything else, consider hiring a house-cleaner. If you keep separate funds, have him pay for it. If your husband is happy with this arrangement, don't complain. As long as the work gets done and he wants to hire someone to do it, that should be all right.

If you can't afford to hire a housecleaner and you're still coming home to a second job of cleaning and cooking while your husband is kicking back in front of the TV with a beer, go on strike. Say "You're not doing your share. You're not treating this marriage as if we're a team, so I won't either. It takes two to make up this team." Stop providing all goods and services for your husband. Leave his dishes in the sink, his socks on the floor, his clothes at the cleaners. Stop cooking for him. Don't remove his beer cans from the den or clean up his toothpaste spills in the bathroom sink. And don't be grim about any of it—be matter-of-fact, even cheerful if you can manage it. I know it's going to drive you crazy, but wait it out. Eventually he has to come around, if only because he needs clean clothes and wants a nice home-cooked meal again.

To alleviate your own discomfort during your strike, clean the dirty areas of the house that most disturb you like the kitchen or the living room. Also, accept that if you want to win your husband's cooperation, you'll probably have to lower your standards some. You can't program him to want the stove as clean as you.

One day he's happy, the next day he's a crank.

How does your husband act when he's a crank? Does he pick on you, disappear into the den, yell at the kids? And why is he being a crank? Are times hard at the office? Is he feeling overwhelmed? Is he moody in general?

One of the first things you need to be clear about is that you're not responsible for your husband's cranky behavior (or his happy behavior, for that matter). Women tend to take responsibility for the moods of others. You may blame yourself, try to figure out what's causing the bad mood, or try to fix it. Check yourself on this one; if your husband wants time to himself and you're constantly hovering about trying to make him feel better, you're part of the problem. If this is the case, back off and let your husband have some private time.

If your husband uses moodiness to get you to do something different—for instance, to come home from work a little earlier, to take care of the kids more, or not to complain when he watches basketball for the tenth night in a row—then have it out with him. Tell him that if something is bothering him, you would prefer he tell you directly. If he continues to act like a crank when you do something he doesn't like, ignore him.

This is a good time to explore your own reactions to his requests for change. Is he a crank because he's asked you repeatedly to try and come home from work a little earlier and you've refused out of hand? Is he a crank because you promised you would pay for half the mortgage but continue to spend money on clothes that you can't afford? Have you left him no other option because you are stubbornly refusing to compromise on an issue that could be negotiated?

It could be that he's just a moody guy. Lots of people are. If so, try not to get bogged down in your husband's dark mood. Don't get cranky in response, and don't take it personally—it won't help him and it will make his moods even harder for you to take. You can't force your husband to be a happy-go-lucky guy if he's not that, but you don't have to go down with his ship either.

- Be sympathetic and open to listening, but continue with your life.
- Ask if there is anything you can do, and then go about your business. Don't keep bugging him to share his feelings with you if he doesn't want to.
- Don't pester him to feel better.
- Allow him to have his feelings without competing for center stage. There will be time for you to express your feelings at a later date.
- If he doesn't want to go anywhere or do anything, leave him be, but don't feel obliged to hang out with him. Make plans with your friends to go out or make sure you have things you want to do at home that keep you busy and entertained.

When your husband notices that you are doing your own thing, he will feel relieved and less guilty or responsible for you. He will also feel as if you are respecting his space, which may actually help him to get out of his mood faster. And if your husband is in any way trying to manipulate you with his mood, he will discover that it isn't working. He may find other ways to try and get what he wants, like talking to you.

If during his moody days he yells at your son, complains about the dinner you spent time preparing, or says your comment about the national debt is stupid, then by all means tell him that is not acceptable. "Your moods are your business, but when they overflow into my life or the kids', something has to change."

Tell your husband that you can handle his bad mood and even be sympathetic and give him a wide berth if he owns up to it. Ask your husband to say "I'm in a cranky mood," instead of disappearing into the den and slamming the door or saying "You always leave hair in the sink." Just his acknowledging that he's in a bad mood makes it clear to you. That way he takes responsibility for his feelings.

He knows his unhealthy habits bother me, but he won't change them.

Women tend to take responsibility for their spouse's health and well-being. Unlike you, if your husband is concerned about your weight, it may be because he finds you less attractive, not because he's worried about the state of your arteries. You care about how your husband looks too, but you're more likely to take a nurturing, motherly role toward his health. After all, you worry about what your kids eat. What's the big deal if you throw in a few concerns about him too. The problem is, your husband probably doesn't take well to being treated like one of your kids. If your husband has some bad habits that you're trying to get him to change, rather than appreciating your concern he probably thinks you're a nag or a party pooper.

Let's examine your part. Do you feel compelled to control your husband's behavior? Do you try to control other things too, like the clothes he wears, how much time he spends with his friends, and what he says to his mother? If so, this is your problem, not your husband's. Give the guy a break. You're treating him like a child, not an equal.

Even if your husband isn't resisting your attempts to

control him, don't take that to mean he likes it. He may feel intimidated but resentful. Let your husband make his own decisions and learn to accept them. Learning that you cannot be in control all the time is an important lesson.

If something is troubling you about your husband's habits, by all means discuss it with him. You can say "I'm worried about your health. Your father died of a heart attack and you have high cholesterol, yet you're still eating greasy burgers for lunch every day." If your husband is open to working on changing his behavior, be supportive and ask him if there is anything you can do to help, like helping to prepare healthier meals. You can work on some of this together.

If he is unwilling to change his behavior, you have a few choices:

- You can accept him as the imperfect person that he is. Let go of trying to change him. Stop talking about it or punishing him for it.
- Choose not to be a part of the behavior that bothers you. For instance if he gets drunk every time you go out with Tom and Sally, tell him you don't want to be included in that foursome any longer. If need be, explain that your idea of a good time is not watching your husband moon the homeless from the backseat of a car. But be sure you tell him that it's fine with you if he wants to go out with them alone.
- Stop any actions that support or encourage his behavior. For instance, if your husband's eating habits bother you, you can tell him you're not going to buy snacks for the house anymore. If he wants to bring in Chee-tos, peanut butter cups, and Twinkies, he will have to purchase them himself. In this way you aren't contributing to a habit

you consider harmful, but you're not preventing him from doing what he wants.

Focusing on your husband's problems can be a perfect way to avoid your own issues. Pay more attention to yourself, on what you would like to work on or change. You'll eventually find that working on yourself is far more rewarding than trying to get your recalcitrant husband to change.

I can't get him to go on vacations or to weddings.

If you're married to a workaholic, you probably have a hard time just getting him to come home for dinner at a reasonable hour, let alone go on a vacation. Or perhaps your husband loves vacations, but he avoids family functions like the plague. Of course, you can't force your husband to go anywhere with you, but you can make vacations sound as appealing as possible.

When you talk about vacations, do you say "God forbid you should want to spend time with me" or "Why don't you get a life?"

Maybe you should try saying "Just think: sex on a remote beach in Jamaica. Doesn't that sound like fun?" or "If you could go anywhere you wanted for a vacation, where would it be?"

It's important to explore why your husband doesn't want to take a vacation (if you don't already know). For instance, is he worried about money? Can you reassure him that your finances are all right? Or is it that his idea of a vacation is different from yours? Are you planning a tour of seventeen countries in ten days when he's already exhausted from work? In that case, start small and go with what you know he likes. Go somewhere local for a weekend. Include activities he likes like sitting on the beach, reading, fishing, or hiking. The idea is for him to see that it's fun away from work *and* that the office functioned just fine without him.

What if you have wanted to see Greece all your life and your husband has absolutely no interest? Consider going without your husband. Going with a friend or a tour may not be your first choice, but it's better than not going at all.

One thing most couples learn after some time together is that they aren't joined at the hip. Earlier in your relationship, it may have been threatening if either of you were to suggest being separated for a vacation. Now, it's probably a sign of the health of your relationship if you can do so.

If you come back having had a great time and you refrain from punishing your husband for not going, you may just pique his interest. (But don't count on it!)

Now about those pesky family functions. You may not want to attend your second cousin's wedding either, but if you're like most women, you probably feel obligated— more so than your husband—to attend family events. Again, you can't force your husband to attend a birthday party for his great aunt—and you're on especially shaky ground if he never attended these events before you came along—but you can talk about events like that in a way that he will listen. Here are some suggestions:

- Don't tell him he *has* to go. The truth is, he doesn't have to go.
- Don't nag him to attend every single event with you or try to make him feel guilty.

- Pick your top ten events for the year. These could be family functions, plays, concerts, or whatever. Ask him to attend these with you. Your husband is probably a nice guy; if you limit the functions and tell him which are *really* important for you, he will probably attend.
- Don't tell him he's a Neanderthal if he doesn't want to go to the symphony and opts to watch football instead. Go with a friend and have a good time.

Lots of women get bogged down in what others think, what's socially acceptable. Having a healthy sense of autonomy within your relationship is a must at times like this. What your husband chooses to do should not be and is not a reflection of you. When you go to events that your husband has bowed out of, don't make excuses for him or be embarrassed at his absence. If asked, be honest: "Harold rarely comes to weddings." If anyone questions you further, say "Talk to Harold."

We argue about everything.

If you say "6:05" when your husband tells you the sun is going to rise at 6:00, if he says yes when you say no, if you say "It's not funny" when he laughs at a joke, then it's time for you to step back and figure out why you and your husband are arguing about everything.

Sometimes couples lose the "politeness factor" and treat each other in ways—rude, confrontational, dismissive, angry, impatient—that they wouldn't dream of treating others. There are a number of reasons why this can happen in a marriage. Perhaps you're annoyed that after years of marriage you still haven't made a dent in the way he thinks about certain issues! Or you may be repeating a pattern of communication that you learned from your parents. Then again, arguing is sometimes a habit that many couples fall into without being aware of it. Regardless of the reasons, however, if you change your behavior, there's a good chance your husband's will change as well. The following are some suggestions to help you break the argumentative pattern:

- Agree to disagree. If you constantly argue about politics or religion, for example, suggest a moratorium. Say "We're probably never going to agree with each other on these issues. Why don't we just agree to disagree on them and set them aside for a while unless one of us has a change of opinion." Then if your husband continues to comment about these issues, you can simply say "We agreed to disagree."
- If your husband is itching for an argument, don't take the bait. If he continues to poke, just say "I don't want to argue." Or you can ask "What's really bothering you?"
- Learn to say things like "That's a good point" or "You have an interesting perspective." Yes, you will probably gag the first few times, but it will come easier after a while. In the long run you will avoid a lot of useless arguments.
- Instead of listening for tidbits you can argue about, listen for points on which you can agree and comment on those.
- Change the subject. Say "You know we never see eye to eye on that. Let's go for a walk, or how about a movie?"

If you and your husband are distant and constantly irritated with one another because of arguments about minor, everyday problems—who did the dishes last, who left the porch lights on again, who let the dog jump on the bed—there's a good chance you're *arguing* to avoid *fighting.*

Perhaps you've had a few fights in the past and they were disasters—you slammed doors, your husband screamed loud enough to scare you, you both said things you regret. Now you avoid fighting at all costs. Or maybe you've never had a fight because you just know it would be a disaster.

Many couples are afraid of having a fight. Arguments about daily irritations can go on forever. There's not much at stake. Fighting, however, is a different story. If you and your husband fight, it means you're going to say how you really feel and you're going to hear how he really feels, both of which are difficult for many people. But saying how you feel and listening to your spouse's feelings are essential to the overall health of your relationship. Fighting *is* healthy if you do it right.

Set your ground rules for fighting before you have a fight. Discuss how you can make fighting "safe" for both of you; for instance: no threats, yelling, hitting, or name-calling. You may request that your husband doesn't walk away if you say something he doesn't like. He might tell you he doesn't want the "silent treatment" after you've had a fight. Since the whole idea behind a "good fight" is to get your feelings across to your husband and to listen to what he feels as well, there should be no reason to hold grudges afterwards.

Here are some general suggestions to make fighting productive:

• Be specific. Instead of saying "You don't care about me," say "I'm furious that you were flirting with our waitress at the restaurant" or "I'm angry because you're not doing the household chores you agreed to do."

- Stay with the issue. Argue about one thing at a time. Don't throw in that he yelled at your son yesterday or that he *always* hurts your feelings. In fact, don't use words like *always* and *never*.
- Have a goal in mind. "I would like you to pay attention to me when we go out to dinner" or "I want you to honor your commitment about the chores."
- Listen to what your partner has to say about you. Sometimes what a spouse says is hurtful but true: "I'm angry that you made disparaging comments about me to your mother," "You complain that I don't spend time with you, but when I came home early tonight you called your girlfriend and stayed on the phone with her for forty-five minutes," or "I feel as if you expect me to take care of you."

Sharing how you feel *about* your spouse *with* your spouse and listening to feelings he has about you means you're open to change and personal growth, and that's what relationships—good ones—are all about.

Bibliography

Allman, William F. July 1993. The mating game. *U.S. News and World Report.*

Anderson, Joan Wester. June 8, 1993. Partners in grime. *Woman's Day.*

Baruch, G., and R. Barnett. 1986. Role quality, multiple role involvement, and psychological well-being in midlife women. *Journal of Personality and Social Psychology* 51: 578–585.

Coverman, S. 1989. Women's work is never done: the division of domestic labor. In *Women: A feminist perspective,* ed. Jo Freeman. Mountain View, Ca.: Mayfield.

Eisler, Riane. 1987. *The chalice and the blade: Our history, our future.* Cambridge, Mass.: Harper & Row.

Gibbs, Nancy R. June 28, 1993. Bringing up father. *Time.*

Gray, John. 1993. *Men are from Mars, women are from Venus.* New York: HarperCollins Publishers.

Hochschild, Arlie, and Anne Machung. 1989. *The second shift: working parents and the revolution at home.* New York: Viking.

Klagsbrun, Francine. 1985. *Married people: Staying together in the age of divorce.* New York: Bantam Books.

LaRouche, Janice, and Regina Ryan. 1984. *Janice Larouche's strategies for women at work.* New York: Avon Books.

Lerner, Harriet Goldhor. 1985. *The dance of anger: a woman's guide to changing the patterns of intimate relationships.* New York: Harper & Row.

Meyer, Patricia H. 1980. Between families: The unattached young adult. In *The family life cycle: A framework for family therapy,* ed. Elizabeth A. Carter and Monica McColdrick. New York: Gardner Press, Inc.

Millman, Marcia. 1991. *Warm hearts and cold cash: The intimate dynamics of families and money.* New York: New York Free Press.

Minuchin, Salvador, and H. Charles Fishman. 1981. *Family therapy techniques.* Cambridge, Mass.: Harvard University Press.

Pleck, J. H. 1983. Husband paid work and family roles: Current research issues. In *Jobs and families,* ed. Helena Lopata and Joseph H. Pleck. Current Research on Occupations and Professions Serial, vol. 3. Greenwich: Jai Press.

Reinisch, June M. 1990. *The Kinsey Institute new report on sex.* New York: St. Martin's Press.

Scarf, Maggie. 1987. *Intimate partners: Patterns in love and marriage.* New York: Ballantine Books.

Schor, Juliet. 1991. *The overworked American: The unexpected decline of leisure.* New York: Basic Books.

Tannen, Deborah. 1990. *You just don't understand: Women and men in conversation.* New York: Ballantine Books.

Tavris, Carol. 1989. *Anger: The misunderstood emotion.* New York: Simon & Schuster/Touchstone.

How to Talk to Your Wife

Patti McDermott, M.F.C.C.

CB

CONTEMPORARY
BOOKS

CHICAGO

Library of Congress Cataloging-in-Publication Data

McDermott, Patti.
    [How to talk to your husband]
    How to talk to your husband : How to talk to your wife / Patti
McDermott.
        p.   cm.
    Two books back to back.
    Includes bibliographical references.
    ISBN 0-8092-3682-6 (pbk.)
    1. Communication in marriage.   2. Interpersonal
communication.   3. Marriage.   I. McDermott, Patti. How to
talk to your wife.   II. Title.   III. Title: How to talk to your
wife.   IV. Title: How to talk to your husband : How to talk to
your wife.
HQ734.M4424   1994
646.7'8—dc20   94-20943
                                                    CIP

Published by Contemporary Books, Inc.
Two Prudential Plaza, Chicago, Illinois 60601-6790
Manufactured in the United States of America
International Standard Book Number: 0-8092-3682-6
10   9   8   7   6   5   4   3   2   1

For my husband, George Boroczi.
Still talking—and listening—after all these years.

Contents

Acknowledgments

I want to thank all my clients, past and present, for sharing their relationship issues with me.

I also want to thank my agents, Betsy Amster and Angela Miller, for their belief in me. As well as being my agent, Betsy has been—at various times—my editor, hand-holder, and cheerleader. She's a terrific friend. Betsy's initial encouragement is also what prompted me to write this book.

I'm grateful to my editor at Contemporary, Gene Brissie, for trusting in my vision of this book and giving me free rein to develop my ideas. I'd also like to thank Elena Anton Delaney for doing such a fine job of copyediting the manuscript.

My sister, Joanne Fahnestock, enthusiastically supported me throughout the writing of this book, as she has with everything in my life. Susan Cox shared some interesting ideas about relationships. Annette DiSano listened

and made suggestions during our long walks with the kids. Beverly Engel provided useful feedback after reading parts of the book. During our monthly breakfasts, Alan Fox heard my progress reports about the book and offered his own thoughts and encouragement along the way.

Also, thanks to Kenna Crabtree for patiently answering my endless computer questions.

Finally, I wish to express my appreciation and love for my husband, George Boroczi, to whom this book is dedicated, and for my kids, Scott, Kim, Dylan, and Kyle. I am fortunate indeed to have such a remarkable family.

Introduction

As often as not, my job as a couples therapist usually comes down to translating what spouses are saying to each other. As you have probably discovered, although you and your wife speak the same language, words for you often have different meanings. Take the word *talking*. To your wife talking means talking about *everything*—her feelings, your feelings, your boss's feelings, fleeting thoughts, and problems. For you, however, talking probably means sharing some of your feelings, transmitting information, giving instructions, or discussing events in sports or politics. You're not accustomed to chatting or making small talk. If you say something, it has to have some meaning.

When your wife asks "What's going on?," what she means is "Tell me everything." She won't be content with an answer such as "Nothing" or "It's halftime." She might feel that you're withholding from her or you're not willing to share your day. Then she's likely to say "You never want to talk to me."

In the beginning of therapy, couples resist my interpreting their talk. What each really wants is for me to take his or her side and declare the other wrong. Both men and women expect the other to talk in *their* language.

Let's say your wife comes home upset and tells you about a problem she's having at work. When she's done, you might say "It's not so bad. You can handle it." Your wife, rather than appreciating your remark, might respond with "You don't care about my feelings." From this point the conversation usually goes downhill. Chances are both you and your wife feel misunderstood. This is where an interpreter comes in handy. I would reinterpret your conversations like this:

You: It's not so bad. You can handle it.
Translation: I want to reassure you. By not dwelling on the problem I'm letting you know that I'm confident you can solve it.

Your wife: You don't care about my feelings.
Translation: I feel dismissed, as if my problems are unimportant. It hurts my feelings and makes me angry when you cut me off.

It's disconcerting to try to have a conversation with your wife only to discover that what you consider obvious she doesn't get or completely disagrees with. That's why it's tempting to complain or get support from your male friends. They understand what you mean. It may seem easier to dismiss your wife with statements like "She's an emotion junkie" or "She talks constantly but she doesn't say anything." But by complaining to your friends, you're less likely to persist in trying to understand your wife. Instead you end up reinforcing all those nasty stereotypes.

Gender stereotypes limit the relationship on both sides. For instance, if you always have to be strong and invulnerable because you're a man and your wife has to be nurturing and self-sacrificing because she's a woman, you're going to be communicating to each other over a tremendous gulf and limiting your opportunites for closeness.

Thanks to the women's liberation movement and now the men's liberation movement, both men and women are striving to express all sides of themselves, from the rational to the purely emotional. And for the first time spouses are trying to have intimate relationships, to be friends. This is revolutionary. After all, up until a few decades ago, marriage was more like a contract primarily for having children. Men and women were trapped in rigid, prescribed roles.

Learning to talk to one another is paramount in the process of getting closer. But it takes practice. Current research shows that there are gender differences in communication. That's where this book comes in. Instead of simply criticizing each other or feeling frustrated with each other, you and your wife will each learn how the other communicates. Once you know that, you can actually talk to each other and be understood!

For your marriage to work, you and your wife have to understand and respect each other's differences and be open to changing your own behavior to accommodate your relationship. If, instead of listening to her, you try to push your agenda down her throat (or vice versa) you lose the special gift of marriage, which is true partnership.

Further complicating the situation is the fact that you and your wife probably learned different patterns of talking from your parents. Maybe your father walked away

from your mother in frustration and complained to you, "Women—no matter what you do, you can't please them." Perhaps your wife's mother complained to her, "Men—they think they know everything." Chances are, when you and your wife talk about issues, you may find yourselves saying or at least thinking the same thing.

Every couple comes into a marriage carrying the baggage from their family of origin. The hard part comes when you try to sort out your own baggage from what belongs to your spouse. Patterns that you picked up from your parents are often so ingrained in your way of being that they feel fundamental, part of who you are. But forging a more open relationship requires a willingness to experiment and step out from beyond your old ways of relating. This means owning up to your own foibles and expecting your wife to do the same. Making your marriage work requires honesty as well as compromise and negotiation.

About the Book

How to Talk to Your Husband/How to Talk to Your Wife is designed to supply you with the tools you need to talk to one another. It will help you bridge not only the gender gap but your personal differences in a practical, no-nonsense way.

The chapter titles are the same on both sides of the book, and they cover what I consider the major trouble spots in marriage: intimacy, kids, money, sex, and daily life. Within each chapter I've included several of the most common complaints, concerns, and difficulties and offered several alternative ways to discuss these issues with your wife or respond to her discussions with you.

Intimacy

When asked, most men will say they want an intimate or close relationship with their wives. But the level of intimacy you are comfortable with, and perhaps your way of achieving it, may be different from your wife's. For instance, women tend to equate talking with intimacy. You, on the other hand, may feel intimate with your wife just sitting down and watching TV together.

Since women are viewed in our culture as the intimacy experts, however, you may feel as if you're somehow lacking in this department. In Chapter one, "Intimacy," you will learn how to listen to your wife's needs without feeling responsible for them. Your way of achieving intimacy is equally important and valid, but, in order for your wife to know this, you have to be able to tell her. I discuss ways in which you can share these thoughts with your wife so she knows what she can do to feel closer to you.

Kids

No matter how much you and your wife are in agreement about your kids, you are bound to have different views about some parts of child rearing. Spouses frequently differ on how much nurturing and how much discipline a child should have. Their opinions about how kids should be raised often seem to be set in stone, having been learned or decided long before they got into a relationship.

Chapter two, "Kids," helps you to discuss your point of view with your wife as well as to listen to what she has to say. Learning that neither you nor your wife has to be in total control in raising your children is the goal. Current research suggests that men and women do parent differ-

ently and that, rather than confusing children, mom's and dad's differing styles actually benefit them. (Of course, I'm talking about differences within a healthy range. No parent should accept abuse of children by another parent.) Accepting each other's differences, although difficult, is essential to raising children in a less conflicted home.

Money

Talk about money can quickly degenerate into arguments that get nowhere. That's because money is also a symbol for other things: status for you, perhaps security for your wife. These attitudes affect everything about money—how you spend it and on what, how much you save and in what way. Because saving versus spending goes to the heart of security and power issues, money is a loaded topic that often polarizes spouses.

This chapter discusses how to hear your wife's concerns and how to express your own. If you don't listen to your wife or she you, each of you is likely to misinterpret the other's insecurity as a demand. And it is the insecurity of both you and your spouse that needs to be understood.

Sex

And then of course, there's sex. Men tend to feel vulnerable about the issues of performance; women, attractiveness. It's difficult to talk about a topic that can so easily be wounding, so often couples don't talk about it at all. Some sexual problems that go on for years in a marriage could easily be resolved if only couples could talk openly with each other.

Chapter four, "Sex," suggests a number of ways for you to do just that. How often you want sex and how and

when you like it are all subjects that can be playfully discussed. Many couples simply don't expect their sexual life to change, as it naturally does, over time. When sex is readily available and you have the same partner, certain habits will emerge. At times you might feel like you've fallen into a rut. Being able to discuss those routines, likes, and dislikes is essential to a healthy sexual relationship.

Daily Life

Just living together day by day is stressful to a relationship. Minor irritations can quickly become major problems if you don't talk about them. Also, if you're looking for a way to avoid talking about real issues, getting irritated at the way your wife leaves half-eaten yogurt cartons in the fridge and dirty dishes in the sink can keep you occupied for months. It's easier to have an ongoing battle about who did the dishes or cleaned the toilets last than to talk about whether your needs for love, affection, or support are being met. Most couples are afraid to broach these more serious topics because they don't know how to resolve arguments.

Chapter five, "Daily Life," illustrates ways that you and your wife can resolve pesky everyday issues without getting caught in arguments that go nowhere. You will also learn how to have a "good fight," one that is productive rather than destructive.

How to Use the Book

You can use the book in one of two ways. If you're feeling ambitious, read through the entire thing (both sides), and then reread a particular scenario when that problem comes up for you.

If you're pressed for time, look up a particular problem and save the rest of the book for later. For instance, if you think your wife spends a lot of time with the kids and not enough with you or if you want her to initiate sex for a change, go directly to page 19, "She never has time for me," or page 61, "I always have to initiate sex." Also read the corresponding chapter on your wife's side of the book to get a feeling for what she may be experiencing.

The Big Picture

Improving your communication with your wife will help you in your other relationships as well. Women and men have different tools in their arsenal; instead of expecting your wife to change to fit your frame of reference, why not try adopting some of her strategies? For instance, you may be able to learn from her how to listen without feeling the obligation to offer advice or reassurance.

You and your wife have embarked on an exciting adventure. Striving for an intimate relationship that is no longer limited to strictly "male" or "female" ways of talking will open up a whole new world to both of you. *How to Talk to Your Husband/How to Talk to Your Wife* will help you to achieve both the intimacy and the partnership that you want.

Trouble Spot One:

Intimacy

You can feel close to your wife just hanging around the house with her. You don't have to go anywhere or do anything. You don't even have to be in the same room; you feel good just knowing she's there.

For you, talking is usually a means to an end. You talk with your male friends about sports, politics, perhaps philosophical issues. To feel close to your male friends doesn't require talking about deep feelings. If you have a problem, you try to resolve it yourself. If you can't, you talk to someone you trust who can give you a solution. If you talk to one of your buddies about a problem, you see it as a sign of respect if he simply says "You can handle it."

It's different with your wife. You share more intimate, vulnerable feelings with her, although this is probably not as comfortable for you as it is for her. In fact, you count on your wife to elicit this kind of talking. Your wife, of course, is more than happy to have you rely on her for closeness.

In this way she feels important, needed, and loved.

Women are usually viewed in our culture as the relationship builders, the nesters. So your wife probably feels that it's up to her to create and maintain a close relationship with you. And to her intimacy almost always involves talk about feelings and sharing the small and sometimes mundane details of daily life. She can easily blame herself if she doesn't achieve what she considers to be an acceptable connection with you. For this reason, she might put pressure on you to be more responsive than you're accustomed to be. She may misinterpret your perfectly natural need for independence as a failure on her part.

If your wife pressures you for more closeness than you're comfortable with, however, you may withdraw from her because you feel she's interfering with your sense of freedom—and withdrawal is exactly the behavior your wife is trying to avoid. Finding ways to discuss your differences, both so your wife doesn't feel like a failure and you don't feel overwhelmed, is essential.

Since your wife talks as a way to connect with you, the content of your conversation isn't as important to her as its emotional temperature is. Ideally she'd like you to listen and maybe to pipe in with a similar experience. This is how she feels understood and accepted, and it helps to keep the conversation going.

You may feel closer to her, however, when you're "taking care of her" by solving a problem for her or reassuring her. So your tendency may be to offer advice ("Fire her and hire someone else") or to reassure her ("It's going to be fine. Stop worrying").

But when you give your wife advice or reassurance, instead of appreciating you she may feel that you don't

accept or understand her. She might say that all she wants from you is for you to listen or to share something of yourself. From her point of view, giving advice or reassurance is a conversation stopper; *talking* is what keeps the closeness going. Learning to respond to your wife in the manner she prefers and telling her what you want from a particular conversation is important. For instance, you may tell her that, along with listening and supporting your ideas, you would also like her to challenge your point of view—play devil's advocate—so you can come to the best possible *solution.*

Trying to balance being "the strong man" with being "the sensitive man" in relationships is difficult and challenging for many men. Sometimes you're supposed to be strong for your wife and take care of her, and other times you're supposed to be vulnerable and "weak." You might not trust that she will respect you or have confidence in you unless you keep your worries to yourself, regardless of what she says. When you do confide your concerns, your wife will probably offer you empathy. And although the empathy feels good, you may find it difficult to accept because it implies that you're "one down." If you withdraw from your wife too quickly, however, rather than intuiting your discomfort, she's likely to conclude that there was something wrong with her response. Understanding why your wife responds the way she does and helping her understand your feelings will lead to better communication between you.

In this chapter I talk about the most common communication problems that arise in men's intimate relationships with their wives, as well as some suggestions to help you through them.

I can't just do my own thing, she's always coming after me.

Does your wife want to be with you every waking moment? Does she follow you into the bedroom when you go to read or complain if you turn on the TV set? Are you a selfish oaf or is she a clinging vine? The truth probably is somewhere in the middle!

If you're expecting your wife to blend into your life— for instance, if you still spend most of your time with the guys, bring home lots of work at night, or install yourself in front of your computer after dinner—then no wonder your wife wants more. Your wife needs to feel special in your life. If you've lived alone or with male roommates, you may not be accustomed to the demands of a relationship. You're in one now, and in order to nurture it you need to give it time. Make dates with your wife just as you would your friends. Don't assume that she's happy simply because you're married. Take her out, pay attention to her, give her a small gift, and tell her you're happy to be with her.

Some men say they are driven crazy by their wife's clinging and dependency but sabotage their wife's efforts to expand her social life. For instance, if you're concerned that your wife won't be available for the times when you want her to focus on you, you may purposely tweak her insecurity by withdrawing from her or leaving to be with your friends. If you are pushing her abandonment buttons as a way to control her, then you have only yourself to blame when she panics and comes after you. Figure out what you want from her and ask for it directly. Let's say it annoys you and makes you feel that she doesn't care for

you when she signs up for a yoga class at night, spends time with her friends, or interrupts your quiet dinner to talk to her mother on the phone. Bite the bullet and say so. Don't try to prove how valuable you are to her by threatening to go away.

If you spend plenty of time with your wife and she still reacts to your desire for personal space by clinging, maybe she's focusing too much on your life instead of her own. Women are more likely than men to make their marriage the focal point of their lives. So, for instance, while you may have maintained your interest in outside activities, she may have let some of her outside interests slip. If so, then it's probably threatening for her when she sees that you have a great time when you are with your friends.

Help your wife let go by encouraging her to find interests outside of your marriage. Whenever she expresses interest in something other than you or the relationship, get excited and reinforce her interest. Don't audibly breathe a sigh of relief—even if that's how you feel— because her anxiety level will shoot up again—("Oh, you're trying to get rid of me").

The next time you want some space, don't turn on the TV or disappear into the bedroom to bury yourself in a magazine. None of your guy friends would have trouble interpreting this signal, but your wife will. Women tend to take responsibility for the feelings of those around them, so she won't view your departure as meaning you simply want time alone. Instead, she will assume that you're angry with her. Being clear and stating what you want and why will help your wife let go without feeling that you are abandoning her.

Try some of the following:

- Give her a peck on the cheek and say "I'm tired. I'm going to space out reading my new seed catalogs."
- Call from work and say "Fred wants to play racquetball after work tomorrow night. I thought I'd check with you and make sure we don't have any plans."
- Say "I'd like some time to myself. It has nothing to do with you."

If your wife follows you, demands more of an explanation, gets angry, gets hurt, or starts to obsess about what she's done wrong, reassure her—once. If she panics and gets clingy, peel her off, give her a kiss, and go off to do whatever you had planned. When you return, be affectionate with her and tell her you're happy to see her.

Don't get caught up in feeling responsible for your wife's behavior. If she is dissatisfied with her life, you may feel that it is somehow your fault or that you should fix it for her. Remember that your needs are as important as hers; she has to manage her own feelings. If your wife insists on merging with you, you're well within your rights to hold her in check.

No matter how much I listen, it's never enough.

Let's say you come home from work, you're tired, and you want to settle in with a drink or watching the news. Your wife comes home about the same time and asks about your day. You say "Fine" and she starts chirping away about the sexual comment she overheard her boss make to his secretary, how much work she left at the office undone, and how her friend Molly lost ten pounds eating nothing but

bean sprouts for a week. You start tuning out. Your eye drifts to the TV. Maybe you tell her about the hurricane in India. She tells you about the car wash and the line at the supermarket. Then she says, "Oh, I had a big argument with my sister this morning." You say "Again?" and then "Tonight's the last game of the play-offs." Before you know it, your wife is throwing her hands up in the air saying "You never listen to me."

It's sometimes hard to understand that when your wife talks about her day, she's talking to be close. The topic doesn't matter. So, if you aren't giving her your full attention, even when she seems to be talking about "nothing" she feels as if you are pulling away.

Try another tack. Before she gets going, pat the couch next to you and say "Sit down here with me. Let's watch the news together." Put your arm around her and tell her "This is just what I need—to unwind by watching the news with you." In this way, you show your wife that there are other ways for the two of you to be close.

Perhaps it's the quality of the listening that is a problem for your wife. If you watch your computer screen out of the corner of your eye, interrupt with advice, or make jokes or sarcastic remarks, your wife probably assumes—correctly—that you're not interested in what she has to say.

Either give her your full attention or tell her you can't listen right now and give her a time when you can. Really giving your wife your attention and listening for five minutes is better than pretending to listen for thirty.

If your wife tends to talk more than you're comfortable with, set a time limit. Say "I'd love to listen to your feelings about your sister. I'm good for about fifteen minutes. How about that?"

Maybe she tells you twenty-five little things and just

when you're about to say "Enough" she throws in a big one, like the fact that her company is cutting jobs. Now you have to listen even if you feel used up. Your wife may be unaware that she is not prioritizing, or she may be manipulating you into listening longer. In any case, tell her that you want her to tell you the important events of her day first. Initially her feelings may be hurt, but, if her goal is to feel intimate with you, then your telling her what you want will help her to achieve it. If she is trying to manipulate you into listening to her longer, giving her your full attention will often help this problem. Most people who talk a lot don't feel as if they are really being "heard."

You might try asking her how her day went before she launches into it. This way she feels that you're interested. Put a cap on it by saying "We've got a few minutes before the game. Sit here and tell me about your day."

If your wife told you something yesterday that was important, perhaps about the argument with her sister, follow up the next day. "Did you talk to your sister today?"

Everyone wants to feel listened to. It's too easy to fall into a pattern of tuning out a wife who talks a lot. Then, because she wants to get your attention, she talks to you even more and you listen even less. This is unsatisfactory for both of you, but often neither of you can figure out how to break this cycle. By respecting your wife enough to ask questions and listening intently to her response, she will feel reassured that you care.

I want sex, she wants to hug and kiss.

If you nuzzle your wife's neck or rub up against her, chances are you're looking for a romp. You might be feel-

ing close to her at that moment or you simply like how she looks in her gym shorts. But if your wife hugs or kisses you, it doesn't necessarily mean she wants sex. In fact, if you respond to her in a sexual way, you're apt to get an angry or hurt response. "Why can't you just be affectionate?" she might say or "Why does everything always have to turn into sex?"

Well, it doesn't, but her behavior sure is confusing. Can you help it if you feel aroused when she sits on your lap? Why is she angry when she should be flattered that you're turned on by her? When you were dating you never had this problem.

For you, sex just isn't that complicated. If you feel turned on, you want to do it. If she sits on your lap and wants affection, well, you can give her all the affection she wants while you're having sex, or afterwards. And, it's not that you aren't being sensitive to her feelings; in fact, her very vulnerability may turn you on. Sure, you want to hug her, but you want to make love to her too.

Your wife, however, feels different needs for affection and sex. Women are accustomed to physical affection. For instance, where you might shake hands or give a friend a clap on the back, your wife probably gives her friends big hugs or kisses. Being hugged or held at moments of vulnerability is a sign of real caring. If your wife feels like she wants to snuggle and you respond with sex, she'll probably feel used, misunderstood, or angry that you're putting your needs before hers.

Your wife may not be very good at expressing her needs for intimacy, and so you may be justifiably confused. It's hard for anyone, your wife included, to ask for comfort in a moment of vulnerability. When you're feeling fragile, you don't want to risk rejection or an insensitive response.

Sometimes rather than asking for affection directly a woman will have sex so as to have the physical closeness she's craving, but she will eventually resent it! This, of course, only leads to more confusion.

If your wife doesn't make herself clear, you might begin to feel manipulated. To protect both of you from getting your feelings hurt during these vulnerable moments, tell your wife that you're perfectly happy to give her all the affection she wants as long as she's clear about what she needs. If it's affection she's looking for, tell her to say so. It's not fair to you if she thinks you should just *know*.

If she says she wants affection but then slides her hand up your thigh, call her on it. I know you're thinking "Why should I call her on it when that's what I want?" Well, the reason is that it's important for your wife to take responsibility for these feelings. Otherwise she's likely to blame you later for not being sensitive to her.

But if your wife makes her need for affection clear, don't pretend to be confused about what she's looking for. You know darn well what she wants. If every time she wants affection from you you use it as an opportunity to get sex, she will feel betrayed. Put your sexual needs aside. If you can be there for her when she needs cuddling and affection, she will feel closer to you and more sexual toward you—just not at that particular moment.

Once you and your wife can distinguish between affection and sex, it will free both of you. You might discover that you too can get feelings of pleasure, love, and support by having your wife rub your feet or caress your back. What a lovely surprise for both of you when one day you can say to your wife "Believe it or not, I don't want sex now. I just want you to hold me."

I don't know what she wants.

Although you may want to be close to your wife, it's possible that you feel stymied each time you attempt to. Because your communication patterns are different, it's all too easy to misunderstand each other's intent.

Let's say your wife tells you how tired she is. You respond in an upbeat manner: "You worked harder yesterday than today." Instead of feeling reassured, which was your intent, she gets hurt and replies "You never listen to me." Taken aback you answer "Of course I listen to you. I'm listening to you right now." Even this doesn't assuage your wife but puts you deeper in the hole, because now she replies angrily, "How could you say that? You just don't care." By this time, you're angry or feeling judged, and you give up in frustration. As far as you're concerned, you gave it your best shot and it wasn't good enough. You throw up your hands and say "I don't know what you want."

The problem here is that you're giving your wife what *you* would like. You may think you're being supportive if you minimize your wife's problems by making comments such as "You can handle it," "Don't worry about it," or "It's not as bad as you think," but your wife wants you to listen and empathize.

Instead of trying to find rational reasons why your wife shouldn't feel a particular way ("No, you can't be tired," "Your mother is always a problem. Why should it bother you now?," "Of course your boss respects you. He just gave you a raise two months ago"), listen to what she has to say. Better yet, say "Come sit down over here and tell me about it." I know this is easier said than done. It runs counter to how you would handle this situation with

a male friend or want a friend to handle it with you. But with a little practice, you'll find it easy.

Women have not been socialized as men have to feel embarrassed by having problems or to keep their problems and feelings to themselves. So, if your wife talks to you about an issue that's bothering her and you don't ask any questions, she will feel unloved and devalued. Asking your wife questions and eliciting more talk from her is the ticket. This may go against your grain, but I guarantee good results.

Accustomed as you are to a more solution-oriented discussion, your wife's talk about the same problem over and over (for instance, her critical mother, her disastrous haircut, or her insensitive boss) may begin to sound like complaining. Or, if you have offered advice and she hasn't taken it, you might get frustrated or angry. It's helpful to keep in mind that talking about her *feelings* is often your wife's goal, not resolving an issue. It's best not to give advice in these instances. That way you can more easily offer your ear without the buildup of resentment. If at any given time you're not in the mood to listen, however, by all means tell your wife or put a time cap on it.

It's possible that you can't figure out what your wife wants because *she's* having problems with closeness. Although many women say they want more intimacy from their husbands, it doesn't mean that they're experts at it themselves. The pressure is on a woman to create an intimate relationship. If your wife is at a loss as to how to go about it, she may feel like a failure. You will know your wife is having difficulty if she

- complains that you never listen or talk to her, but when you do it's never done to her satisfaction

- encourages you to talk about your feelings and then later criticizes you for not being decisive enough
- says she wants to talk or have your attention when you're already late for work, heading out to play tennis, or watching the biggest basketball game of the year, then feels rejected and withdraws when you don't jump at the opportunity.

If this is the case, help her out. Be direct with your wife. Ask her specifically what she wants from you. Point out (lovingly) that her bid for closeness always comes at a time when you're busy or leaving the house. Tell her you don't think her timing is an accident. Tell her you would like to be closer to her, but that she's making it very difficult.

If she asks you to be more intimate than is comfortable for you, say so. The more direct you are with your wife, the less she will be able to blame you for *her* problem. Eventually she will be clearer as well.

I want to be closer with my wife, but I don't want to be overwhelmed.

The old myth that women take away a man's independence by marrying him is deeply ingrained in our culture. Men are often fearful that when they get into an intimate relationship they will lose their freedom. Every couple must wrestle with the issues of autonomy versus togetherness. Finding a balance between their desire for separateness and their desire for partnership is one of the hardest tasks a husband and wife face in a relationship.

Although both you and your wife want an intimate relationship, your comfort zones may be different indeed.

13

Each person has his or her own rhythm; spouses constantly drift from feelings of closeness to feelings of separation. This creates problems, of course, if you or your partner doesn't understand the other's pattern or respect the other's comfort zone.

In general, women thrive on more intimacy and being intimate for longer periods than many men are comfortable with. For some women, intimacy is like a cozy nest, one she's not in a big hurry to leave, especially when the relationship is going well. Men find the nest lovely too, but after a time they get antsy. They want to do other things: hang out with the guys, putter. And often it's this difference that leads to confusion and conflict.

For example, let's say you spend a marvelous Saturday with your wife—you're close, you have fun, you have great sex. Come Sunday morning you're ready to see the guys, play some golf, or putter around in the garage. To you, this behavior is perfectly natural. You've had a great time and your relationship is in fantastic shape. What better time to go on about the rest of your life?

Your wife, however, finds this behavior completely mysterious. *She* would never leave when the going was good. Her tendency would be to leave if something were amiss. In that case, she might withdraw from you, go out with her friends, or try to talk about what's troubling her. Instead of understanding that you're different, your wife assumes that you want to leave because something is wrong or she couldn't fulfill all your needs. When you come back and "pretend" nothing is wrong, she will be disturbed. Instead of welcoming you back with open arms, your wife is withdrawn, pouty, or angry. This in turn confuses or angers you. You might think "What more does she want?," "She wants to control me," or "Does she expect

14

me to spend every waking moment with her?" Suddenly that cozy nest starts feeling like a prison. From this point on, you and your wife are at cross-purposes: She's trying desperately to get you back into the nest, to fix whatever she did wrong, and you're running the other way. This scenario is a common one in many marriages and is easily resolved by a discussion about your differences.

You will benefit from explaining to your wife that the more independent you feel, the more love you have for her because you can give it freely. Reassure your wife by telling her that, when you want to do other things, it's because you feel filled up with love and closeness. You leave feeling good and come back feeling even closer.

Your wife may also be threatened because she knows that you can spend a whole weekend bird hunting, all of Friday night playing poker, or all day playing basketball and barely mention her. The camaraderie and companionship you feel with your friends is different and is a welcome change from the intimacy of your relationship with your wife. But she takes this behavior personally; your perfectly legitimate need for space is perceived by your wife as a need to escape her.

Of course your wife experiences a need for space too—it just looks different. When your wife goes out with her friends, more often than not they talk about their relationships with spouses, kids, and coworkers. So, although your wife wants space as well, the relationship usually remains her focus.

Help your wife understand that your need for distance rarely has to do with her directly. Explain that you simply are different from her, but it doesn't mean you love her any less. If you do, she likely will not punish you or be angry with you when you bounce back ready for more intimacy.

Trouble Spot Two:
Kids

Of course you love your kids, but you never expected them to take over your life as much as they have. This is the lament of most parents. You may be having more difficulty than your wife with the financial, emotional, and time sacrifices that your children require. Men have not been raised, as most women have, to take care of children. It's still usually girls who babysit neighbor kids and help their mothers take care of brothers and sisters. So your wife may not have been as surprised at the amount of time and work children require, but you sure are. Not only is this difficult for you, but your wife may not be as sympathetic as you like. In fact it seems to you that she now finds your baby's eating and elimination habits more interesting than she finds you.

You may have been thrilled to have kids—couldn't wait to get involved. Maybe you were determined not to be like your father but instead be a real participant. But every time you pick up the baby or try to talk to your son about

his abysmal grades, your wife corrects you. Suddenly she's the expert and you can't seem to do anything right.

Current research argues that men and women have distinctly different parenting roles, that there is no reason for you to become "another mother," that a father's contribution is unique. Your touch is firmer, you're probably not as tuned in to your kids' everyday emotions and problems as your wife is, and you make more demands on them. You expect them to do their best in whatever they try, and you push them harder than your wife might. Let's say you and your wife are at your son's tennis tournament. You get irritated when you discover that your son is "overly fair" when it comes to calling his own lines. You make a point of telling him that it's not a smart way to play the game. Your wife, on the other hand, may feel proud of her son because he's so concerned about being honest.

It's true that while many women tend to focus on the emotional status of their children, men are often focused on the practical picture: how will my children fare in the world? You worry that your wife's coddling will leave them unprepared to handle all the curves that life will throw them. You know it's tough out there, and you want your kids to be prepared. What may sometimes come across to your wife as criticism or as a demand on the children is really just your way of showing you love them and want the best for them.

Being a father is difficult because the roles of fathers are changing. Wanting to be involved with your kids is now socially acceptable; however, you're still under pressure to be a good provider for them. And, your boss, although he or she may give lip service to your interest in your children, won't think much of you if you leave a business meeting to attend a Little League game or your daughter's

school play. The reality in most companies is that you will be passed by for promotions if you choose to spend time with your kids rather than staying late at the office with your coworkers.

In order to give up the financial and emotional perks that come from being on the fast track, you need strong support and encouragement from your wife. But, even though your wife has probably told you over and over that she wants you to be involved, she may subtly (or not so subtly) undermine your feelings of competency. That's because she's conflicted too. She *does* want you involved, but she is scared by the thought of giving up or sharing control of the kids. The less secure your wife is in other areas of her life the more she will get her ego satisfaction from being a mother. Her insecurity will make it difficult for her to share child rearing with you.

And, as committed as you are to being a good father, you still think you deserve a life of your own. You want to have time for sex, friends, and vacations without the kids. You want a night out with the guys. You want your wife to pay more attention to you and your needs. But you don't know how to say all of that to her so it comes out wrong, or at least she hears it wrong. She says you're selfish or that you're rejecting her and the kids. Right about at this point, you begin to have fantasies of going out for a paper and not coming back. And then your wife takes you out for a romantic dinner and tells you you're a great husband, lover, and father. Your son comes and sits on your lap and says he loves you. You're a willing participant again.

Men have more opportunities now to spend time with their children and participate in day-to-day family life. You can show affection and nurturing with your kids in ways

18

that weren't acceptable for men to in the past. But this is a new world for most men *and* women. It will take some practice before you feel at home in your new fathering role. In this chapter are some of the issues that come up for men along with some ways to go about talking with your wife about them.

She never has time for me.

Before you and your wife had kids, you had good times together—and maybe some great sex. At the drop of a hat, you could go out and see a movie or just watch TV. Back then, you were number one to your wife. But when you had kids, her allegiance shifted. Now it seems her love, interest, and concern flows toward the children, and you're left out in the cold. You want to go to a movie; she's taking the kids to a matinee. You want to make love; she's too tired. You finally go out to dinner and she spends the whole time talking about your son Arthur. You suddenly think "I don't have a wife anymore; I have a mother."

You might be assuming your wife wants or chooses to be with the kids over you when she might feel she has no other choice. For instance, if you're not participating or helping, she may be overloaded with taking care of the kids. It's possible she resents you for not being involved or for resenting *her*, and this makes her spend even more time with the children.

If you're expecting your wife to be there for you in the same way she was before you had kids, your expectations of your wife are too high. Demanding that she spend time with you without helping her to make the time is self-defeating.

If you withdraw or complain that your wife is spending too much time with the kids, she will undoubtedly feel criticized. She won't understand that your complaints arise from wanting to be with her more. She will assume the *opposite*: you don't want to be with her. Instead of going off to be with your friends because you feel deserted by her, say how you feel. Tell her that you feel left out and that you miss her. If she is delighted but says she can never find the time, try one of the following:

- Instead of eating a hurried meal with the kids, make a date with her for a quiet dinner after the kids have gone to bed. Bring in take-out food so neither of you has to do extra work.
- Suggest that you get a babysitter one night a week. If you can't afford a sitter, ask a family member or neighbor to babysit for you and you do the same for them.
- Meet for a long lunch when the kids are in school.
- Get away for a weekend.

If your wife resists all these suggestions, she's probably using the kids as an excuse to avoid you. She may feel uncomfortable straddling the roles of mother and wife. Many women abandon their wifely role when they have children, often because they feel less attractive. You can help or hurt her self-image by what you say.

- Don't say that ever since she started hanging out with the kids she lost 40 IQ points.
- Don't talk about how cute your secretary is.
- Don't approach her solely for sex; approach her also for conversation and affection.
- Call her by her name, never Mom or Mommy.
- Reassure her that you find her attractive.

- Insist on sharing nonkid things together. When you go out, don't talk about the children.

She may be avoiding you because there are other problems brewing in your relationship, problems neither of you are addressing. For instance, if she's angry at you because she feels like you never listen, she might indirectly punish you by spending more time with the children.

If you suspect or know that other things are going on under the surface, bring them above the surface. Insist that she talk about what's troubling her. Make sure you let her know you're interested in what she's feeling. Of course, this implies that you're ready to confront the problem yourself. Letting her know this might help her to bridge her silence and open up to you.

She's too easy on the kids.

Are you worried that your wife is creating kids who won't be strong enough to thrive and succeed in the world? This is a concern that many fathers share, especially those who feel that their wives "coddle" their children. Rather than seeing your point, it's more likely that, if you think your wife is too easy on the kids, she probably thinks you're too hard on them. You will be encouraged to know that, regardless of all the talk about both parents having to agree on every detail of raising kids, your kids can benefit from both parenting styles. However, if you're like most parents, you and your wife each think you are right and are more determined to change the other's behavior than to accept it. Suggest to your wife that you both try to back off and allow the other the space to parent differently. You may

both be surprised to note that your kids, rather than being confused, actually thrive.

Usually, though, it's not that easy to do. Letting go will be difficult for your wife, as she will judge much of what you do as too harsh, critical, or insensitive. It will also be hard for you to let go if you think her softness is spoiling the children or making them too weak to function well in the world.

But if you try, it might work something like this: when your son brings home a dismal report card, your wife might focus on what went wrong, and you might focus on making sure it doesn't happen again. Both reactions are valid, and your son will get something from both of you.

If you and your wife can't come to such an agreement, your behavior or hers is probably more extreme. Let's take a look at your behavior. Is your wife easy on the kids because you're too hard? Are you reacting to your kids using a pattern you learned from your family? Perhaps you're more negative or critcal than you realize. If you picked up this habit from one or both of your parents, you might not be aware you're doing it. If this is the case, your wife is presenting you with an opportunity to work through some of this automatic parenting. Instead of fighting her or telling her she's the one with the problem, ask her to help you. Whenever she hears that critical or sarcastic tone, she can signal you with a wink or mention it to you later.

Perhaps you're worried that the kids like your wife more than they like you. Do you feel left out or unimportant when the kids go to her for advice, comfort, or conversation? This may have to do as much with the image your kids have of you as it does with your wife's easiness.

22

Make yourself more available to the kids. Don't wait till they approach you: talk to them and ask them questions. If you show interest in their lives and offer support and encouragement, not just hard advice and criticism, they will be banging down your door to hang out with you. You might find that your wife becomes threatened by this shift. Include her by telling her your plan. Say "I would like to be closer to the kids" or "I'm going to make a point of talking to the kids for a short time every evening."

On the other hand, if your wife is insecure about her role as a mother and if she's more interested in being your children's friend, she's probably not disciplining the kids consistently. If she's afraid that her kids won't like her if she says no or that other people will see her as too stern, she will give in to them constantly. Instead of criticizing her or getting into the same old arguments about discipline, try being supportive of her firmer, more adult, secure side in the following ways:

- Form some rules that both of you can stand by. For instance, agree that whenever the kids ask to do something unusual (not just riding their bike to the supermarket), each of you will say "I'll discuss it with your mom/dad and get back to you."

- Always back up any disciplinary action your wife initiates. In this way she's reinforced for holding the line with the kids.

- When your kids ask for something, turn to your wife and say "What do you think?" In this way, you model for your children respect for your wife's opinion, you engage her in a joint decision, and you make her feel like *your partner* rather than one of the kids.

She makes me out to be the bad guy.

If your wife says things like "Wait until your dad gets home" or "Your father is going to be angry about that," then she's living in the past. This is a throwback to an era when women were supposed to leave disciplining the kids to the men. It's definitely not fun to come home from a long day at work only to hear your wife recite a litany of complaints for which you are supposed to mete out punishment. This is not a healthy alternative for your wife either, as it undermines her position with your kids.

The first thing to consider is whether you're encouraging her to act like this. Do you insist on being the disciplinarian when the family is together? Are you convinced that you know best? If you want to be looked upon as a wise, all-knowing, strong father, then you must also take the heat when it comes to discipline. If you insist on being "the man of the house" and keeping tight control, then you have no one to blame but yourself when your wife makes you out as the bad guy.

If your wife doesn't have equal authority, she may give in to you, resenting you all the while. She may also form an alliance with the children against you as a way of getting some power for herself. For instance, she may say things like "Well, if it were up to me you could go, but of course we know your father's going to say no." She may even go one step further and say something like "I tried to convince your dad to let you go, but he said 'Absolutely not.' And we know he's the boss."

If you don't want to be perceived as the bad guy any longer, share the authority with your wife. This may not be as easy as it sounds because your wife plays as big a part in

this pattern as you do. Your wife isn't taking the responsibility for parenting. With this program she can criticize you when things don't work out. For instance, when your older son starts talking back, bringing home Cs instead of Bs, and pummeling his younger brother, she can say, "Well, no wonder. You were so strict with him" or "He's very angry with you."

Discuss the situation with your wife. Tell her that you want her to do the disciplining for events that occur on her watch, just as you will take care of those on yours. Then agree on what actions you will take for certain behavior. Tell the children together. In this way, your wife will naturally align herself with you instead of with the kids.

Perhaps in making you the bad guy your wife is criticizing you personally. In other words, you can't do anything right. In that case, this is a relationship problem, not a kid problem. If your wife is feeling angry at you for other things—not spending time with her, not listening to her, or not giving her affection—she may find it safer to make an alliance with the kids to hurt you than to say how she really feels. If you think that's going on, confront her directly. Say "If you're angry with me, spit it out."

It helps to pay more attention to your wife. Do things together. Make her feel connected to you rather than in cahoots with the children. Encourage her to talk to you about what kinds of disciplining she had to do; discuss the children as if you were a team. Soon you will be.

She's always complaining about the kids.

Does it seem like the only thing your wife ever talks about is the kids? And that she never has anything good to say?

Maybe she calls you up from work to complain about how the morning went: Amanda couldn't get dressed fast enough, Bradley wouldn't eat his breakfast, and Maryanne refused to open the bathroom door so Amanda could pee. She bitches about having to drop off the kids' library books on her way to work and complains about having to rush home to cook dinner.

What kind of response does your wife get from you? Do you do any of the following?

- tune her out, and just say "mmmmm"
- tell her you have more important things to do
- interrupt her with some advice

If you're responding in any of these ways, you're contributing to the problem. What you have now is a chain reaction. Your wife senses that you're not listening. She doesn't know how to get you to listen other than to amplify her complaints. If you listen and support her feelings (you don't have to do or say much) the chances are good that she'll complain less.

Believe it or not, your wife may be complaining about the kids as a way of being close to you. Her complaints may be a way of communicating. To you this might seem like a pretty weird way to have a conversation, but for your wife it's a way to share feelings with you. She doesn't know that by complaining so much she's pushing you farther and farther away. Give her a little help.

- Give her five minutes of real listening. Remember, she's trying to get close to you by sharing her day. After a while, you might even throw in a few complaints of your own.

26

- Ask her what she would like from you. A hug? Some advice? Just to listen?
- Ask how her day went before she has a chance to complain. For instance, call her up and say "Did Amanda get it together a little faster this morning?"

If none of this lightens your wife's burden, if she doesn't respond by complaining less, perhaps she's feeling overwhelmed. Most of us don't like to admit when we feel overwhelmed, and your wife is probably no exception.

You can offer to help in a number of ways if your wife is having a difficult time. Offer to take over for a few mornings, or take the kids out to the park on the weekend to give her some time to herself. You could also suggest bringing in some help, perhaps a babysitter one day or evening a week. You can also lighten her load in other ways, such as bringing in more take-out food, sending out the laundry, or getting the kids to help with some chores.

If you've tried everything and she still complains, tackle her negativity straight on. Say "I've tried everything I could to help, but you're still complaining. What do you suggest I do?" Perhaps she's imitating some behavior that she learned from her mother. Even if the behavior seems frighteningly familiar to you, don't say "You're just like your mother." (If you haven't discovered it yet, this is definitely not something you want to say to your wife!) Instead, comment on it without invoking her mother: "You're usually not a negative person, but you seem more so when you're around the kids." If your wife doesn't get it, then the next time you're around her mother, comment on her mother's negativity. "Boy, your mother really is negative, especially with her kids and grandkids."

I can't talk football with a baby.

It takes time for men to grow into their fathering roles. If you expected yourself to be a perfect father right off, you might feel disturbed at your lack of connection with an infant. When you thought of fatherhood, you might have envisioned throwing baseballs to your kids in the backyard, bicycling with your kids, watching football with your kids, or looking over the boys who come courting your teenage daughter. You weren't prepared to hold and nurture a tiny newborn.

According to some current research men and women have different "parenting tools" in their tool kit. For instance, mothers provide more nurturing in the early infant stages, and fathers focus more on their children's futures and success. So it's natural and comfortable for your wife to use her parenting— nurturing—tools right away and conversely hard for you to access yours—giving advice or guidance. You feel at odds about what exactly you should be doing with a three-day, three-week, three-month, three-year-old baby. How do you talk about college, business, the Super Bowl with a newborn? Well, you can't, but don't get discouraged. Your special skills will become more and more useful as your child matures.

Many men feel uncomfortable handling babies. They're so small and fragile, and you feel so big and bumbling when the baby disappears in your arms. Because of this, you might be afraid to dress your baby or change your baby's diapers for fear that you will hurt him or her. Your wife may exacerbate this problem by insisting that there is only one way to change a diaper or by hovering over you anxiously every time you pick up your child.

28

Perhaps you could learn a few things from your wife but find this role uncomfortable. If you're accustomed to being in charge at the office, being an "intern" at home may be unpleasant. But if you're barging ahead and taking charge without knowing what you're doing, you're going to upset your wife, and she's probably going to respond with criticism.

If you talk to your wife about your fears and insecurity, I'd wager she will be delighted to give you a hand and reassure you. If you come to her for help, it reinforces her trust of you. She'll know you wouldn't just go off and do something with the baby without checking first. You have to remember that part of her parenting tool kit includes her being protective of her baby—sometimes too much so when it comes to you.

Once you learn to comfortably handle the baby, it's important that your wife let go. If she continues to hover and offer advice, at some point it becomes her problem. You and your wife will always have different parenting styles. The sooner you both accept this, the smoother your child rearing years will be. But be sensitive to your wife's concerns; she's probably not out to get you. She's simply trying to be a good mother.

For instance, if your wife tells you that your baby, perfectly happy being rocked on your shoulder, likes to be rocked on his stomach instead, you could simply say "He likes my shoulder right now, but I'll move him down if he gets fussy," instead of "Here, you take the baby. I'm going over to Larry's."

If she insists on being the expert, tell her that you will handle your son or daughter in your own way. Reassure her that if you need advice or help, you will ask for it. If she tells you that there is only one way to burp, change,

stroll, or hold the baby, tell her you've just discovered another and perhaps she could learn from your technique.

I didn't expect to have to change diapers.

Many men figure that the bottom line is their wives should take care of the children, especially the babies. Even if your intentions were to share the workload, it all feels different now. After all, she's a *mother.* You think she should act like one. You're willing to help, of course, but there's no doubt that the main contribution should be from your wife.

Well, welcome to the nineties. If your wife is at home and the agreement is that she does the work at home, then you're *partially* off the hook (women who stay home need relief too). Otherwise, it's time to face facts. If your wife is working outside the home as you are, then fairness dictates that you share the work at home. If your wife is asking, or by now insisting, that you share in the duties of parenting, including (YES!) changing diapers, it's time to get with the program. Most men still get away with doing less, however, so I assume you aren't going to give in that easily.

In order to avoid helping out with the kids at home you may say things like

- You warm up the bottle better than I do.
- I don't know how to buckle Buddy's shoes.
- You can load the washer faster than I can.

If your wife buys these flimsy excuses, don't be surprised if she begins to comment on your competency in general. She may actually believe your argument, or perhaps she just finds it easier to do things herself. The price you pay is

she'll view you as an incompetent person. For instance, if you can't change a diaper or help your ten-year-old with his homework, why should she listen to you when you suggest a different approach to a parenting problem?

If your wife is secure enough, however, she won't let you get away with excuses like the ones listed, or with even better ones. She will continue to talk to you about sharing the workload, and she'll get increasingly angry or disappointed.

Taking control of the situation might feel better. Instead of waiting for your wife to drag you into participating, why not volunteer? Choose the jobs that are the least distasteful to you and suggest that you take them over. If you can't stand changing diapers, offer to bathe the baby in the evenings, make dinner, or take over doing the laundry.

Many husbands feel that the contribution they make as the major breadwinner is not given the credit it deserves. If you're putting in more hours at work than your wife, then this is true for you. But you need to go back to what you and your wife discussed before you had children. Did both of you agree that you would work more? If so, your wife should indeed make adjustments for your extra workload and not expect you to come home and put in as many hours with the children as she does.

Because fathers' roles are in a period of transition, you are vulnerable to being told what's expected of you. Chances are, because you can't use your own father's role as a guide, you can be talked into believing that nothing but absolute devotion to the family is acceptable. Women, more than men, are tempted to give up having any life other than parenthood, especially in the beginning. If, after you have your child, your wife insists that "the family

that's stuck together stays together," she's the problem. If your wife is criticizing you and trying to make you feel guilty for wanting time away, be firm and insist that you have the right to pursue outside interests. Also, suggest that she does too.

Talk concretely about what's expected of you. If she asks you to do more than you feel up to, try not to complain, withdraw, or get angry. Remind her that you're tired, that you've had a longer day than she did, and that you deserve to sit down. If she talks about how much work she has to do, sympathize with her. If you have some extra energy, volunteer to do something more than usual. Remember that you are a team. Working together is the goal, and that means sharing both the joy and work of raising children.

Trouble Spot Three:

Money

Many men still see their most important role in a marriage as that of provider. Currently it's accepted, assumed, even expected that wives also work. However, the *ultimate* burden of financial security still sits squarely on the shoulders of men. That is, it does in the eyes of most of society, including, probably, most of your male friends. Being a good provider is not only your "job," it's hooked up to your ego and it puts you in competition with other men. Men measure status based on who is most successful. Making more money than your brother, friends, colleagues, or tennis partners means that you are more successful than they.

For your wife, money is more likely to represent security than status. She wants to know that the kids will be able to go to a good college, you'll have enough for a comfortable retirement, and you'll be able to take decent vacations. Her status is derived from relationships; she's

more likely to judge herself a success or failure depending on how close her relationship is with you. If you buy her a new Porsche, for instance, to her (and probably to her friends), it is a sign that you love her. For you it validates your role as provider supreme.

Although you may see your primary role in the family as a provider, your wife may feel that your role as nurturer is equally or even more important. She may push you to give more time to your family because she values the emotional commitment you bring to the relationship. If she tells you that she wants you home more or that you don't spend enough time with the family, however, you might take that to mean that she doesn't appreciate what you are contributing to the family financially. Being able to talk about what each of you considers a priority is important so as to avoid misunderstandings.

Not only are you and your wife likely to attach different symbolic meanings to money, you might also have different priorities when it comes to how money is saved or spent. Since no two people regard money in exactly the same way, you and your wife are bound to disagree about what to do with what money you do have. For instance, how much should you save? What is your idea of a good investment? Gold? Stocks? Real estate? Hiding money in Switzerland? And what do you want to spend your money on? Do you want to buy a new car? Does you wife want to buy new living room furniture?

For your wife, deciding together how you spend your money is part of how a good relationship works. You're a team. You, however, may not be so accustomed to working toward a consensus, and so you may find it discomfiting to report to your wife about what you're spending money on.

To you this might feel like an infringement of your independence, your freedom.

If you make more money than your wife, you may feel you should have more say about what happens to it. Perhaps you think she should consult with you before making a purchase even though you wouldn't dream of telling her before you buy a new set of golf clubs. Your wife, however, may insist that your relationship is an equal partnership regardless of who makes the most money. She may put pressure on you to consult her about decisions that you previously made on your own.

Or you may find yourself with the opposite problem on your hands: a woman who assumes that it's your responsibility to provide for her. If you once agreed you should but now feel pressured about this arrangement, you have to find new ways to talk with your wife to encourage her to take equal responsibility in the marriage.

Although men usually make more money than their wives, there may come a time when your wife earns more than you. This will undoubtedly be a difficult transition for both of you. Your ego may be bruised, you may question your role in the family as the provider, and your wife might walk on eggs because she's worried about your feelings— or her own. Any reluctance you have to talk about your feelings has to be pushed aside, because, if you don't discuss this issue, it will surface in other areas of your relationship. For instance, you may argue about how to discipline the children, who left the dirty dishes in the sink again, or why you dislike your wife's friends.

Because men are supposed to be strong and because their self-image depends to a large degree upon how successful they are, it's often next to impossible for them to

share money or job worries with their wives. If you buy the notion that men should handle their problems themselves, you may find yourself alone. You must bridge your feelings of inadequacy in order to talk to your wife and get the support you need.

Talking about money issues is important to the health of your relationship. In this chapter are examples of some concerns you might have and some suggestions on how to begin a dialogue with your wife about them.

She thinks money grows on trees.

When you were first dating or married, your wife was ecstatic when you bought her expensive gifts or took her out to trendy restaurants. Maybe you loved the way she showed up for each date in a sexy new dress and thought her "Shop till you drop" bumper sticker was funny.

Now she no longer buys a new outfit every week, but you have more placemats, knickknacks, and ties than anyone could ever use. Your kids look like an advertisement for Neiman Marcus, and your wife is constantly telling you to update your wardrobe.

If you expected that once you settled down your wife would read your mind and instantly embrace your goals for saving money for the future, you're being unreasonable. If the rules have changed since you were courting, you have to say so. Otherwise your wife is likely to feel that you don't care about her anymore. And instead of embracing your goals, she will see your complaints as proof that you aren't giving.

Because moneymaking is tied to your ego, maybe it's

hard to say no to your wife. It can trigger your feelings of inadequacy: "If I were really a great guy, she would be able to spend all the money she wanted." Some men get alternately angry and amused at their wives' spending habits. One time you might be furious when she walks through the door loaded down with purchases and tell her she's selfish or out of control, or that she needs to go to a support group for compulsive shoppers. The next time, however, you may treat her like a cute little girl when she shows you a new dress or yet another set of flowered dessert plates. In either case, chances are she's not going to take your call for change seriously unless you give her a compelling reason to change her behavior.

For example, do you have goals for saving your money? Do you have hopes for a home, vacations, retirement? Share these goals with your wife and elicit her help in reaching them. Make it more palatable by having short-term as well as long-term goals. Tell her "As soon as we've put away $5,000 toward our retirement, let's save $2,000 and go to Hawaii."

If you and your wife argue about money all the time, your arguments are probably masking the larger issue of who's controlling whom. Accustomed to being on her own prior to marriage, your wife might find it difficult to "answer to someone" about her spending. She may resent being told how much money she can spend or not spend. Instead of hearing you as her partner, all she hears is that you're trying to control her. You'll know this is the case if she

- screams "You can't tell me what to do!"
- rushes out to the nearest mall and buys six pairs of shoes just to show you

- refuses to tell you how much money she is spending

You, on the other hand, will know you're reacting paren-
tally if you are likely to respond with comments like

- When are you going to grow up?
- I make more money, damn it, and you will spend it the
  way I say!
- You're a spoiled brat.

As long as you and your wife see money as an issue of who
is controlling whom, you will never resolve the practical
issue of how much you have and how you want to spend it
in a reasonable way. Instead of trading insults, approach
your wife as an *adult* and suggest that you both stop name-
calling. Have a discussion about your differences with the
goal of reaching a compromise.

- Try writing down how much money you both earn and
  how it's being spent.
- Try making a budget you both can live with. This probably means allowing more discretionary income than
  you would like and less than your wife would like.

Chances are if you don't feel like partners when it comes to
how you spend and save your money, you don't feel like a
team in other areas of your relationship as well. Stick with
this project until you can hammer out a compromise.
You'll find it will gradually bring you and your wife closer,
and you will eventually operate as a team.

She expects me to tell her
every time I spend a penny.

In order to help you figure out why your wife is so interested in how you spend every penny, let's take a look at

38

how the two of you handle money together.

Maybe your wife used to think it was romantic when you would spend every dime of your paycheck for a surprise trip to Puerto Vallarta. She laughed when you christened your new house by breaking a two-hundred-dollar bottle of champagne against the fireplace, and she was overwhelmed with love when you bought her a bracelet that you couldn't afford. Now she nags you about the mortgage payment being late, gets livid if you come home with two surprise tickets to a Guns N' Roses concert, and gives you the evil eye if you spring for drinks at your local pub when your favorite team wins.

If you've got plenty of money in the bank and the bills are being paid on time, then you're right: your wife's got a problem. However, if you still insist on new jet skis, two-hundred-dollar bets on every football game, or impulsive vacations to Palm Springs when your kids need shoes, it's time for you to grow into your marriage and your family. If your wife yells that you're irresponsible and makes sarcastic remarks like "The neighbors are taking up a collection for the boys' school clothes" or "You don't give a whit about this family. All you care about is yourself," your wife is making it easy for you to blame her for the problem. When she reacts in this way, you can dismiss her as a nag, a bitch, or a drag. Instead of seeing your wife as the problem, you need to change some of your spending habits. It's easier said than done, but there's no way around it.

If your wife is demanding minute details about how you're spending money, perhaps she's insecure about her place in your life. If you used to spend money on her and now spend time away from her and spend money on your friends, she may feel that she's not important to you anymore. In this case, it's not an issue of money, but of time,

love, and affection. If you are out of the habit of buying your wife a gift, taking her out to dinner, or simply saying "I love you," make her feel special again and she will stop complaining.

If your spending is well within reason, then perhaps what seems to you like an overweening concern on your wife's part is really just her way of saying she wants to be involved in the financial decision making in the marriage. If you have continued your old pattern of spending what you like, when you like without consulting her, she probably feels that you don't trust her or don't respect her opinion.

To your wife, a partnership means talking about what each of you is doing. If you come home and triumphantly announce that you moved money from your joint money market account a month ago and put it in some stock you'd been keeping your eye on and now it's making a bundle, instead of congratulating you, your wife may well be annoyed. From your point of view, you made a solid, informed decision. From her point of view, you discounted her input. Taking your wife's feelings and opinions into consideration is not only fair, but it will also lessen her anxiety and her anger.

The pressure is all on me.

If you've got money worries, it may be difficult for you to talk to your wife about them. Men are still supposed to be *strong.* So although you can talk to your wife about your job to a certain extent, when it comes to the deeper issues—competition, vulnerability, being unsure of your decisions—you're probably tempted to keep those feelings

closer to the vest. But if you feel alone with this pressure, you could start resenting your family.

Since you don't talk about how you're feeling, your wife may not realize how overwhelmed or pressured you really feel. When she shows you the new dress she bought or complains that she wants to quit her job because her boss is a jerk, she has no idea that her comments make you feel even more pressured, inadequate, or resentful. If you react by being sarcastic or if you withdraw, your wife will think she has done something wrong. She won't know what's really bothering you.

One question to consider is where the pressure you feel is coming from. If you're driven more by internal forces than by the actual needs of your wife and kids, then it's important not to blame your wife for your drive to succeed. You can still talk to her, however.

Saying something simple like "The pressure at work is really getting to me," is likely to open up a conversation. Chances are your wife will be happy that you're sharing your feelings with her and will be open and supportive.

Sometimes, however, women find it difficult to understand the depth of men's drive to succeed. Women generally view the workplace as an extension of family; they look to their boss or coworkers for approval or friendship and work toward cooperation rather than competition. Men on the other hand see the workplace in gladiator terms, as an arena for competition. If you tell your wife your concerns about work and she says "Don't take it so seriously" or "Aren't you worried that your colleague will stop liking you?," you may not feel inclined to open up again soon. But resist the temptation to withdraw. Instead, hand her this section of this book and ask her to read it.

Better yet, talk to your wife about the strategies of the workplace as you see it. If your wife is a working woman, she can benefit from understanding how men operate in the work environment.

Pay attention to your own tone of voice as well. If you want your wife's support, don't make her feel you're complaining about her and the kids. Don't say "I'm too busy working to pay off his orthodontia" when your wife suggests you both attend your son's soccer play-off. Make clear exactly where the pressure is coming from: "If I lose this Gillicuddy account, I'll lose my Christmas bonus" or "Jones and I are neck and neck for this promotion."

If you feel unappreciated, say so. Don't disappear into the den with a paper or the TV remote control. If your children are lucky, they won't have the burden of worrying about money. But sometimes giving children that gift they've been asking for places an extra burden on you, because you may feel taken for granted. Everyone wants to be appreciated for their efforts. If you're not getting enough strokes, ask for some. Say "I'm working hard. I'd like to know you and the kids respect/love/appreciate me for that." Just talking to your wife about your feelings can lift the burden. If your wife is caught up in her own pressures at home or at work, she may sometimes forget that you need strokes too. Jog her memory.

If it's your wife who's putting pressure on you to make more money, the situation requires a different response. If you're doing the best you can and your wife isn't working, urge her to get a job. If you're both working already but she's feeling pinched, sit down with her and see if there are any ways for you to increase your disposable income by compromising.

Perhaps your wife is anxious and doesn't express her feelings well. Although it seems to you that the pressure to support the family is all on you, your wife probably feels pressure as well but in a different way. In fact, she may feel more helpless, because she is not able to contribute monetarily as much as she would like. Keep in mind that the average woman still earns 33% less than the average man. If you think your family's future rests in your hands, I imagine your wife feels the same way. Sit down and talk about it. If you can come to appreciate your wife's concerns without feeling personally attacked and your wife can come to appreciate the pressure you feel not only to take care of your family but in a competitive sense as well, you will be on your way to a closer relationship.

She expects me to take care of her.

Even these days, some women expect to be taken care of. Usually they marry men who comply, at least for a while. If your wife is dependent on you now, she's probably been this way all along. Both you and your wife have been benefitting from this strong man–helpless woman relationship. Chances are, just as your wife finds it difficult to be strong, you have probably found it equally hard to be vulnerable. But within any relationship people change. If you now feel able to show more vulnerability or feel more secure about yourself as a strong person, you don't need another to reflect that for you. You're ready for your relationship to accommodate that change.

If you've grown tired of your role, it's up to you to gently inform your wife that you feel it's in her best inter-

est to become more independent. As with anyone, the more independent your wife becomes the better she will feel about herself and your relationship.

Of course your wife may not give up her dependent role willingly. If she says things like "Oh, all these mutual fund statements and telephone bills look alike" or "You're so much better at dealing with bankers than I am," don't buy it. But don't get hostile or sarcastic either. It's safe to assume your wife is going to need a lot of encouragement. Being hostile or sarcastic will undermine any attempt you make to help her become independent. Simply reply that you have faith in her ability to understand.

Talk about your bills and investments with your wife. Insist that she listen and understand where your money is and what you're doing with it. Make a budget together. Expect that she will live up to her responsibilities in the budget. Treat her like an equal and she will start to act like one.

If she asks the same questions over and over, suggest that she take notes. Ask her to go to the bank, call your broker, or pay the monthly bills. Your wife may feel threatened by your request to get more involved in your financial life. Since she thought that your taking care of her meant you loved her, she may now feel that you no longer love her. Reassure her that in fact it's because you do love her that you're now insisting that she play an equal role. Tell her that if something happens to you, you want her to be prepared rather than to be helpless at a vulnerable time.

Don't be surprised if you feel twinges of ambivalence as you move toward a more egalitarian relationship. As much as you want this transition, once your wife begins trusting her own decisions, you might feel threatened

or even angered by her burgeoning independence. At this point, you may begin to give her some mixed messages. For instance, you might elicit her opinion and then criticize what she says. In the long run this will defeat your purpose. So be aware of this tendency and do your best to encourage your wife even in the midst of your own insecurity.

She's making more money than I am, and I don't know how to handle it.

When a wife starts making more money than her husband, it upsets the balance of power and takes some adjusting on both sides. If you're having a hard time accepting this new turn of events, chances are your wife is struggling as well, either because of her own adjustment or because she knows that it's difficult for you.

Part of how you respond to this situation will depend on how you both reacted if previously you made more money than she did. If it was irrelevant then, it will be easier for both of you to adjust now. However, if you thought that because you made more money you deserved more power in the relationship, then your wife may be tempted to dish out what she used to receive.

If you recognize in her some of your own previous behaviors (for instance, making financial decisions without consulting you, questioning how you are spending certain monies, or criticizing some of your decisions), call her on it, as she should have done to you. If she retorts "You didn't consult me when you were making more money," say "I realize that, but you didn't speak up for

yourself. That doesn't mean I should do the same." Reassure her, however, that if the tables are turned again, you will remember what it felt like.

If your ego is tied to moneymaking, this turn of events will be difficult for you. You've been socialized to believe that you would be the one to carry the ultimate responsibility for your family's financial success or failure. In learning to cope with this new situation, there are traps you should avoid falling into:

- Don't withdraw from your wife. This will create distance between you and make it harder to cope with this new situation. Your wife may be reluctant to approach you to talk if you're withdrawn. She will instead pull away from *you*.
- Don't make sarcastic comments about her job, boss, or career. If you are feeling angry, say so. It's natural for this situation to make you uncomfortable, but blaming your wife won't help.
- Don't back away from discussions about money. For instance, if your wife asks your opinion, don't suddenly say "Well, it's your money. You decide."
- On the other hand, resist the temptation to boss your wife around just because you're feeling insecure. Your wife might even go along with this behavior if she's feeling guilty or confused, but eventually this dynamic will feel false and make both of you resentful.

If you can open the topic up for conversation, it will make the transitions easier for both of you. Since your wife may hesitate to approach you for fear of hurting your feelings, show her you are capable of coping with the situation. Help her make the transition by letting her know you're on

her side. Encourage her to do well, and let her know you're interested in her career. Applaud her achievements.

If the idea of discussing your feelings with your wife makes you uncomfortable, try a little bit of humor. Present her with an "executive key" to your bathroom. Or say "We would make the perfect poster couple for NOW" or "Does this mean you won't cook my favorite, chicken cacciatore, anymore?"

She doesn't know how worried I am about my job.

If you have bought the notion that the financial future of your family lies squarely on your shoulders, it will be very difficult for you to share your fears about losing your job or being demoted. If your self-worth is wrapped up in how well you take care of your family, then you probably assume that your wife will judge you as you judge yourself— as a failure.

Not only are you supposed to take care of your family, you are expected to carry the burden of doing so stoically. Men are conditioned to carry their fears within; talking about them is viewed as a sign of weakness. Women on the other hand feel more comfortable baring their souls without being concerned that doing so makes them one down. Because of this difference, sensing something is wrong, your wife may be pressuring you to tell her what's going on. As far as she's concerned, it can only get better if you spit it out.

You might feel you're in a double bind: on the one hand, your wife wants you to admit your vulnerability, but you also know that she expects you to be strong. Given

these two conflicting messages, sometimes not talking about what's really going on seems like the safest and most comfortable way to go.

However, if you don't talk to your wife, your concern about your job is sure to surface in other ways. For instance, you may pick fights with her, complaining about food being wasted or shoes being worn out too fast. You may take any stray comment she makes such as "Oh, look at that big house, isn't it beautiful?" as a sign that she finds you lacking.

Many men reason that they are protecting their wives from bad news or from worrying by not telling them what's going on. However, you're not doing your wife any favors by not talking to her. She would probably prefer that you tell her how you are feeling so she can offer you some support. Otherwise, she's likely to take your bad mood personally and wrack her brain trying to figure out what she did wrong.

Of course, you're thinking you know exactly what's going to happen if you tell her you're worried: she's going to get worried too. Then you have to contend with not only your own feelings but hers as well.

You don't need to feel obligated to reassure her that everything will be okay. She's a big girl. She can feel anxious and still survive, and so can you. If her anxiety starts spilling out—for instance, if she constantly ruminates about what's going to happen—be direct and tell her that her anxiety is making the situation harder for you.

If she questions you too much, say so. Tell her you're not comfortable talking about the situation all the time but you promise to keep her informed of any new developments. Just because talking makes her feel better doesn't mean you can't put limits on it for your own comfort.

You may be worried that you will lose face if you admit your fears to your wife, but chances are you will earn more love from her when you are vulnerable and share your feelings. Although you might not share these kinds of self-doubts or concerns with a male friend or colleague, remember that your wife wants to know how you feel and feels closest to you when you tell her.

Trouble Spot Four:

Sex

When women think or talk about sex, they use words like *passion, romance, love, connection*. If you're like many men, however, sex for you is a bit simpler: you see your wife waltz by in her tight jeans and you want to do it. And, contrary to your wife's lofty descriptions, the words that come to your brain are likely X-rated.

Men get sexually turned on visually more than women. For instance, you probably notice dozens of women throughout the day—at work, on magazine covers, walking down the street—and momentarily feel a sexual buzz. Your wife can turn you on simply by crossing her legs a certain way, wearing a tight T-shirt, or perhaps breathing.

Although you might knock your wife's socks off when you stride across the room bare chested, more than likely it's talk and a feeling of closeness that really turn her on. Feeling important and cherished is perhaps more important to your wife than the sexual act itself.

When you feel that sexual buzz, you want to have sex.

There is no time lag. Your wife, on the other hand, might want some conversation first, some intimacy before leaping into bed with you. You may think back to your earlier days and remember a time when your wife didn't seem to need so much time or attention. But the reason "Let's do it" worked for you when you were dating is that your wife invested those words with lots of meaning: "He's crazy about me" or "He's got to have me." Now she feels that you're saying exactly what you mean—that you want to do it. When she stops hearing romance in those words, she will stop responding to them in the way you want her to.

For you sex might seem like a good, fun way to bridge any distance. Your wife however may need to feel connected to you before you have sex. So, if you both go to bed angry from an argument and in the morning you suggest making love, your wife is likely to say no. Instead of appreciating your effort to break the ice, she may be hurt and say you're not considering her feelings.

It's hard for you not to feel rejected if you suggest sex and your wife says no, and the same goes for when you say no to her. Some men get caught up in feeling they should always be ready. You might worry that your wife will find you weak or unmanly if you don't try to satisfy her whenever she wants sex. But, every married couple eventually realizes that they both won't always want to do it at the same time. Learning to say no and accept no in a loving way is essential to a healthy relationship.

When communication is poor in a marriage, sex can be used to drive a message home. If you or your wife has difficulty talking about what's bothering you, it's sometimes irresistible to use sex as your battlefield. For instance, if you feel that your wife spends too much time with the children and none with you, you may act out your

anger by refusing to have the kind of romantic sex your wife likes. If your wife feels emotionally neglected by you, she may withdraw from you sexually rather than talk to you about what she finds missing in the relationship.

During the course of your marriage you, your wife, or both of you will probably have some type of sexual problem. For example, it's not uncommon for men to have trouble getting or maintaining an erection at one time or another. If your wife gets upset or concerned and pressures you to talk, this could make matters worse. Her own fears of being unattractive may surface, and in the midst of your own anxiety you may feel you have to reassure her. Your simply saying "I don't want to talk about it just yet" is perfectly understandable. Most erectile problems are transitory, and the less attention paid to them the better. However if the problem continues, it's better for you to bring it out in the open so that your wife can help you cope with it. (Any sudden sexual problem, unless clearly linked to anxiety in your mind, should be checked out medically. Frequently what seems to be a sexual problem turns out to be an easily resolved medical one.)

If your wife has a sexual problem, you might feel as if you should fix it. Or it may trigger fears in you that you are inadequate as a lover. Men are susceptible to believing that their wife's sexual enjoyment is their responsibility. Of course it is not; it's up to your wife to tell you what she likes. It's also her responsibility to talk to you about her problems and to find ways that you can help her overcome them.

In this chapter are the most common concerns I hear from husbands and some suggestions on how you can talk to your wife about them.

She never wants to do it.

Is she saying no because you're pressuring her to have sex more often than she is comfortable with? If you want sex twice a day and she's a twice-a-week gal, then you're going to be rejected most of the time. Asking over and over will either annoy your wife or make her feel inadequate, neither of which is going to elicit a resounding yes the next time you ask.

Maybe you end up getting a guilty yes from your wife for every three nos. This pattern is guaranteed to make both of you feel less than excited about the sex: you, because you had to jump through three hoops to get it; your wife, because she still feels pushed into having sex.

Instead of complaining or continually asking, have a discussion about the frequency you each prefer and then compromise. Be direct: "I'd like to have sex twice a day if it were up to me. What about you?" Your wife may say "Well, I'd be comfortable having sex twice a week." You might compromise with four times a week.

Sex, just like all the other aspects of your marriage, involves compromise. Just because you like to have sex twice a day doesn't mean you get to push your wife into doing it. On the other hand, your wife could give a little, too, and please you by having sex more frequently than she's accustomed to. If in doubt, make the national average your goal. This will probably mean that you will have to scale down your number and your wife will have to up hers.

Maybe your wife is saying no because you ask at inopportune times. For instance, if you grab her boob and give her fanny a squeeze when she's unpacking the groceries or when her mother is in the kitchen, she's going to turn you

down. Ditto if she's just told you she's exhausted from work and wants to go to sleep. Pick your moment. Or better yet, ask her when she likes to make love—mornings, evenings, or lazy afternoons?

How about the way you ask? Maybe she's looking for more romance, some flowers, a dinner date. Perhaps you've been taking her for granted and haven't been thinking about what she would like. Instead of leaping on her as she's undressing, saying "How about it?" five minutes before she's supposed to leave for work, or complaining that she never wants to do it, surprise her with a small gift or ask her to dinner.

If you have been asking and your wife has been refusing for some time, then chances are by now your wife doesn't even know when she *wants* sex because she's too busy fending you off. Back off and give your wife a chance to approach you. You'd be amazed how well this approach works if you give it enough time.

Saying no all the time takes on a different meaning if your wife is using rejection and withdrawal as a way of hurting you for other complaints she has. By continuing your pattern of asking, you're helping her avoid talking about what's bothering her. Because you both stay focused on sex, the real issue never surfaces.

Whatever she's angry about can't be any worse than the situation you already have. If you know there's a problem and you've been attempting to override it by having sex, forget it. Instead of asking for something she has no intention of giving, ask her what's bothering her. Tell her you're interested in how she's feeling. This indicates a willingness on your part to listen to what she has to say. You may find that once your wife feels like she can talk and

you will listen, she will open up sexually once again. Once she opens up to you and knows that you are willing to listen to her feelings, gently remind her that you would like her to be more direct in the future.

What's wrong with wanting plain old sex? I can't help it if I'm not always in a romantic mood.

You probably had more romantic sex with your wife when you were wining and dining her during your courtship and early on in the marriage than you do now. Even your quickies had a passionate edge to them; perhaps you dared her to do it before her roommate got home or you steered the car onto some dark street, pulled her to you and said "I can't take it another second. You're driving me crazy."

Of course there's nothing wrong with sex plain and simple. Sometimes you just feel aroused and want to satisfy the urge. It's not romantic, it's a physical desire. If she would just cooperate, it wouldn't take long to satisfy it. But most of the time, your wife won't be content to have that kind of sex. Women like passion. That's why women read romance novels and why you "read" *Playboy*.

Because your wife is less likely to separate sex from love, she rarely thinks of having sex in order to relieve a momentary urge. If what she's looking for when she asks for romance is closeness, then sex for sex's sake will disappoint her. Perhaps if you give your wife what she wants—cuddles, some long romantic conversations, a little whipped cream here and there—she won't resist or resent your interest in just plain old sex.

Think back to your last half-dozen sexual encounters. If most of them were the way you like them, simple and to the point, then it's time to give your wife what she wants as well. Some men are uncomfortable with romantic sex. But a lot of women are uncomfortable with unromantic sex, so you just have to compromise.

On the other hand, you shouldn't be blackmailed into having to throw gardenias all over the bed every time you want to make love. If you have to come up with a new two-hour romantic scenario every time you want to have sex, then your wife is being unreasonable. Let her know what kind of romance you are comfortable with. In other words, kissing her for twenty minutes is okay, but talking like Rhett Butler is not.

Play a game with your wife. One time she gets to tell you what she wants—maybe it's being wined and dined, then whisked up and carried to a candlelit bedroom. Next time you tell her what you want: "Let's do it standing up in the hallway, like, right now."

If your wife is uptight about sex, she may be putting up barriers by making unreasonable demands for romance. In this way she doesn't have to examine her own reticence. If you feel like your wife is making it impossible for you to please her, it's time to talk to her. Tell her flat out what you're feeling. "I'm jumping through hoops just to have sex with you, and you're still turning me down. It's time to talk about what's going on with you."

Sometimes, of course, a couple gets lazy and stops working on their relationship. Just wanting plain old sex can be a sign of that laziness. Keeping sex interesting in a marriage can be a challenge, just as keeping your whole marriage interesting and vital is a challenge. Variety and compromise are the key.

I don't know how to please her.

I rarely hear women say that they don't know how to please their husbands. They usually know exactly what turns them on. Whether they do it or not is another issue, but they almost always know their husbands' triggers. That's because most men are more direct about what they like and how they like it. It also doesn't hurt that it's easy to tell when they're aroused.

It may not be so easy with your wife. She may have difficulty telling you what she wants. Worse yet, maybe she doesn't know what she wants but was hoping you did! Many women have a harder time being specific than men. If your wife has trouble telling you what she likes—*and* if she has difficulty reaching an orgasm—then you're left guessing.

It's frustrating if you want your wife to enjoy sex as much as you do but she won't help you out. Some women are insecure and feel uncomfortable if they take "too much time" getting pleasure. Your wife may be tempted to satisfy your needs and not focus on her own because of this kind of embarrassment. She may even fake more pleasure than she's feeling so that you won't continue to focus attention on her. Of course, you probably see right through that.

Tell her that it's important that she get pleasure too. Say you're willing to take as much time as necessary to help her feel good. Once she feels safe with you she will be able to relax, and that should move things along.

The best way to insure that everybody is having a good time is to talk about it. Share your fantasies, and ask your wife to share hers. Ask her if there is something she would like you to do that you haven't thought of yourself.

Ask her what she likes or what she thinks she might like. Don't let her get away with responses like "Whatever you do is fine," "Everything feels good," or "I don't know."

Say "I'll tell you what feels good to me, and then you tell me one thing that feels good to you." If she can't verbalize what she likes, then during sex you can say "That feels good to me" and then "Does this feel good to you? Here? Or here?" Do some experimenting: read some sex books together or see some films.

Is your wife not shy, but critical? If no matter what you do she gets frustrated or criticizes you, then she's blaming you for her inability to relax or have an orgasm. She needs to take responsibility for her own pleasure. You can get her to do this in a couple of ways:

- If she says that if you would just touch her right she would be okay, ask her to be specific. Tell her she has to let you know what feels good.
- If she's still complaining or frustrated, suggest she show you what feels good while you watch. Tell her you can learn best at the feet of a master, so to speak.

Perhaps you're too concerned with pleasing your wife. If you're worried about your performance—whether you're doing a good job, whether she's enjoying herself—you're probably not having such a great time yourself. Maybe she's having a fine time, but you need to be reassured because of your own insecurity about sex and about your ability to make her happy. Both men and women worry about how they rate in bed. Although technical prowess comes in handy, it's not the essential ingredient for pleasing most women. Loving, nurturing, cuddling with, and caring for your wife will get you a lot more points in bed than how long you can keep going.

Sometimes focusing on yourself will actually enhance your wife's pleasure. If she knows you're having a good time and not *trying* so hard then she can relax too.

She won't try new things.

Do you remember a time when your wife was more fun, less uptight? Perhaps before, if you said "Let's do it in the elevator" she might not have said yes, but she would have at least giggled about the possibility. Now, if you suggest such a thing, she just shakes her head or pretends she didn't hear you.

Perhaps your wife felt freer before because you paid more attention to her. You were both caught up in the excitement of a new relationship. You focused solely on each other. If she felt loved and safe, she was probably willing and interested in experimenting with you. Try putting some romance back into the relationship now. Take your wife out for a romantic evening. Dinner, a long talk, and holding hands may rekindle her interest.

Sometimes women feel they should behave a certain way as they get older or simply because they're married. So perhaps having sex in the backyard was okay when you were just married, but it's unseemly now. If you have children, your wife may have taken on the role of mother and partially left behind her sexual self. If *you've* fallen into the trap of relating to your wife solely as a mother or as your wife, try to adjust *your* attitude.

- Buy her some sexy underwear.
- Tell her she looks sexy.
- Don't call her Mom or Mommy.
- Come to bed showered and smelling nice.

59

- Give her a kiss at the most unexpected time and tell her you love her.
- Give her a big smooch in front of the kids. She may be embarrassed, but she'll love it.

Let your wife know that you're attracted to her and that you find her sexually exciting. She's not about to try a strip tease for you if you tell her she's getting fat, how much younger she looked five years ago, or how great your secretary looks. Be willing to make yourself vulnerable too. If you want her to strip-tease for you, why don't you show her how it's done? If you can make sex playful on your end, perhaps she won't worry so much about how she looks.

Maybe your wife is willing to experiment, but she's just not interested in the same games you are. If you want your wife to greet you at the door dressed in fishnet stockings, six-inch heels, and a hat, she may not feel comfortable. However, she may like having massage oil rubbed all over her or like rubbing it all over you.

If you've been asking her to participate in a specific sex act and you keep getting a no, ask her what she likes. Is there anything she'd like to try that you haven't done yet? If you don't reciprocate by doing stuff she likes, she might not be willing to try what you want.

The routine of a marriage can actually make couples shy with one another. Sometimes it even seems it would be easier to try something new with someone else. That's because there's safety in routine; you both know what to expect. If you're ready to experiment sexually and get out of your routine, try encouraging your wife in ways that make it fun to try new things, once again.

Go away for a weekend. Play one of the adult movies

in your hotel room. Say "Remember when we were dating and you did those kinky things with the frozen daiquiris?" Jog her memory about the good times. That should give you both a few ideas.

I always have to initiate sex.

From adolescence on, you've probably been initiating sex. That's because in our culture it's the man's job to pursue sex, and the woman's job to say no or yes. That's a hard pattern to change once you're married. Maybe your wife feels just as stifled by that pattern as you do. Or maybe she's just abdicated her sexual feelings to you and doesn't think about it. But you're absolutely right to feel stifled; there's no reason why the man should always be the one to initiate. Before you talk to your wife, however, check your own behavior. Perhaps you're approaching your wife so often that you don't give her a chance to initiate. Accustomed as you are to this role, you may not be giving your wife any time to allow her own sexual feelings to bubble up. If this is the case, back off a bit and see what happens. She may surprise you.

If your wife doesn't take action on her own once you've given her the space to do so, then tell her you would like her to initiate sex sometimes. Tell her it's crazy to assume that she only wants sex when you do—which is true. Then, don't turn her down when she makes a move. If your wife is not used to initiating, she's obviously not accustomed to rejection either. If you want her to continue initiating, it's a good idea to be interested the first few times. If you turn her down, do it in a loving, reassuring way.

Some men say they want their wives to initiate sex, yet

sabotage their wife's efforts every time. If you've been asking your wife to initiate but always end up turning her down, you're giving her a double message. Although the idea of your wife being more aggressive may sound good, it can be threatening, too. Even if you've never had performance anxiety, you might be stricken with it when you're suddenly expected to perform at someone else's whim. Instead of being turned on, you might find yourself feeling insecure.

Maybe your wife does try to initiate sex, but she does it so shyly that you don't get the message. For instance, if she says "I'm going to take a shower so I'll be nice and clean," you might not realize that your wife is hinting that she wants to have sex. The same goes if she says "The kids won't be home for another hour." If your wife is afraid of rejection, she will issue these invitations in ways that are obscure so that she won't feel bad if you don't pick up on the hint. She may also be hinting in vague ways as a way for you to gracefully not pick up on the message. In this way she may think she's protecting your ego or saving you from having to reject her. But if her message is too subtle for you, say so. When in doubt, ask. "Are you suggesting we make love?"

Being romanced is fun. Tell your wife you like to feel seduced too. You had to overcome your fears in order to romance women. There's no reason why she can't overcome any fears she has. Playing the seductress may not come naturally to your wife; she may have to learn how. Whatever attempts she does make to seduce you, don't make fun of them. One joke about her at this moment will throw her back into not initiating again.

Of course, she will initiate in her own way. For instance, she may plan a romantic dinner or a walk on the

beach or reach over shyly for a long kiss. Your best bet is to respond to her initiation in a like manner. For instance, if she gives you a long smooch, don't instantly stick your hand down her pants; return the kiss and take it from there slowly. If you want her to initiate, be willing to let her guide you the rest of the way as well.

On the other hand, simply making the first move might be all your wife can manage for now. If this is so, then give her some help by taking over; if she's shy you don't want to overwhelm her. Once she sees how receptive you are, however, she can gradually increase her participation and perhaps—to your delight—it won't be long before she's orchestrating the whole works.

I know she's not enjoying it, but we don't talk about it.

Not being able to talk about this problem only exacerbates it. Yet instead of talking many people clam up when sex isn't going right. It's understandable—almost everyone feels vulnerable when it comes to sex. You are, after all, literally exposed in bed, and it's easy to be hurt or feel rejected. Don't let that stop you. Bring it up. If your wife won't talk about it, then it's up to you. Be direct. Say "I don't think you're enjoying sex." Talk with her about it until you understand why.

Remember that, while you might feel vulnerable about your performance, your wife is likely to feel vulnerable about her attractiveness. If she thinks that you don't find her attractive, she may have withdrawn from you sexually. Give your wife a lot of encouragement, compliments, and attention. Don't make comments about how gorgeous your former girlfriends were, and don't make derogatory re-

marks about your wife's body—not even if you think you're just being cute.

Whatever the problem—difficulty relaxing, trouble having an orgasm, not enjoying certain parts of sex—she may not know how to talk about it. Telling you that something hurts may be something she can't get herself to do. You might help her by asking her if there is anything you could be doing that she would enjoy. Or if there is something you are doing that she isn't comfortable with. It's not fair to you, however, to be put in the position of trying to guess what will make your wife sing. Tell her that you want to help her to enjoy sex, but that you need her help.

Perhaps she's afraid of hurting your feelings. Women have been trained to believe that men will fall apart if they make any comment at all about a man's sexuality. So your wife may be treading lightly around an easily resolved problem just to spare your ego. Maybe she doesn't realize that you would be glad to do things differently if it would please her. Let her know that sex is a two-way street for you. Tell her you will enjoy it more if she enjoys it. She may not react right away, but as time goes by, she may feel more and more comfortable being open with you.

If you've given your wife every opportunity to tell you if something is troubling her and she insists that everything is hunky-dory, then believe her. She may be having more fun than you think or at least as much fun as she feels comfortable with. Tell her you expect that she will tell you if she's unhappy or wants you to do something differently. Then get back to paying attention to your needs and your sense of fun.

Perhaps your wife is withholding her pleasure from you out of anger about other issues. If this is the case, she

needs to find a healthier mode of communication, like talking. You might point out to her gently that, since she's not having much fun, it seems she's cutting off her nose to spite her face. Tell her that you understand talking must be extremely difficult *or* she must believe that you won't listen if she does talk if withholding sex is the only way she feels she can get a message across. Encourage her to tell you what's really going on and assure her that you're ready to listen.

Trouble Spot Five:
Daily Life

One of the biggest challenges in a marriage is simply managing to live together day by day. On the good days, you feel connected and happy to be together, you read each other's thoughts, and laugh at each other's jokes. On the bad days, you and your wife can argue about everything—how many covers you like on the bed, whether the dog should be inside or out, and what you want for dinner.

The way spouses react to the differences between them often changes over time. Maybe you used to love the way your wife had opinions about everything and held her own with your friends. She thought your friends were fun even though she didn't agree with them. Now you get irritated because you think she takes issue with everything, and she says your friends are way too conservative. If you can learn to handle your differences with humor or acknowledge them without being critical, you and your wife can enjoy each other's company once again.

Do you sometimes feel as if you've become one of your wife's pet projects? Some women seem to pay more attention to their husband's behavior than their own. And once they start noticing, the campaign to change you isn't far behind. For instance, like many women, your wife may seem obsessed with your manners—or what she deems your lack of them. She considers what you put in your mouth; whether it's good for you or not; and how you chew, drink, digest, and burp all worthy of comment. Ditto for talking too loud or otherwise behaving in a way that causes her embarrassment.

You too are annoyed by some of her behaviors—she talks too much, she gives air kisses to women she hates, and after years of marriage she still gets embarrassed when you pee with the bathroom door open. But you don't assume your wife will change; usually you just tune her out. Your wife, on the other hand, thinks it's her job to change you, especially when it comes to such things as eating habits, politeness, and cleanliness. Women feel it's up to them to mold those they love; you are her work in progress.

Your wife may also feel obliged to coerce you into attending cultural events and family functions, yours and hers. Women generally tune in to family obligations more than men. If you didn't go to your cousins' weddings before you got married and now your wife is telling you that you *must*, there's bound to be friction. Compromising on these issues can dispel the tension that arises every time a family event comes up.

If you and your wife are having a tough time in other areas of your relationship but you don't talk about it, then you're likely to find fault with her everyday behavior. For

instance, you might be steaming inside when she turns you down again with "I have a headache," but instead of saying "We need to talk about our sex life," you complain that she left makeup all over the bathroom sink again or say that you don't care how cold she is, you're sleeping with the window open tonight. By arguing about these petty issues, you and your wife never have to look at the big picture. You can stay annoyed with each other indefinitely. Many couples find this constant low-grade irritation more comfortable than just having a big blowout argument. You've probably never learned how to have a good, healthy fight, and so you both avoid the "big" conflicts at all costs. Learning how to have a productive, rather than destructive, fight is fundamental to a healthy relationship.

It doesn't really matter what the daily issues are that get to you and your wife; what matters is how you handle them. By talking about the normal stresses and strains of living together, you can avert the tension and resentment that build up when these issues aren't dealt with.

I'm not insensitive—she's too sensitive.

At work you like to be direct and say what you mean. If something's wrong you want to know about it so you can fix it. You assume that other people operate at the "facts level" as well. At home, however, you might find that this approach doesn't work very well. If your wife complains that she's gained ten pounds and you say yes when she asks if you noticed, don't be surprised if she's devastated. Ditto when you tell her that her new haircut is not as nice as the old one or if you point out that the sweatpants she's

wearing aren't very flattering. From your perspective, you're just trying to be helpful. From her perspective, you're being critical and giving her proof positive that you don't find her attractive anymore.

It makes perfect sense that your wife would react this way. In our culture young, thin, attractive women are the ideal. Your wife probably feels as if you are constantly insensitively pointing this out to her. Often women would rather live in a world of half-truths. Both of you may well know that your wife has gained ten pounds, but it makes her feel good to think that you love her enough that you don't even notice. (Anyway, how much weight have *you* put on?)

On the other hand, if your wife's insecurity makes her hear criticism, disapproval, or insensitivity where none is intended, you probably feel as if you're walking in a mine-field all the time. If she assumes every comment you make—"I like your sister's new haircut," "John and Susan joined a health club together," or "I've gained weight . . ." is a comment about her, tell her in a neutral tone "I was talking about so and so. If I want to comment about your looks, weight, or hair, I'll do it directly." Repeat this same response every time your wife gets hurt by a comment you happen to make about someone else. And do your best not to monitor or censor your conversation to appease your wife's insecurity. If you don't cave in to your wife's problem, eventually she'll be able to listen without such unhealthy sensitivity.

If your wife complains that you're insensitive because you still call her at the last minute to say you're going out for a beer with the guys or to tell her you've made plans for both of you to meet friends for dinner, then she's right.

Consulting with your wife is a sign of respect. She's not a coworker, buddy, or roommate; she's your wife. She wants to feel included in your life—especially when it impinges on hers. Make the effort and call ahead of time or ask her opinion before you make plans for both of you. At first it may be uncomfortable, but after a while it will come naturally.

Perhaps you're worried that if you're not direct enough with your wife—about her weight for instance—she won't change her behavior or realize how much a problem bothers you. So you complain or get a little sarcastic when you talk about her weight. Your reasoning says that if you're supportive and "dishonest" she won't get it and she will gain even more weight because she's convinced it's okay with you.

But the truth of the matter is that complaining or being sarcastic won't get the results you want. Trying to control anyone's behavior with criticism doesn't work. The person just gets resentful, angry, secretive, or rebellious.

Just as your wife has to decide eventually to accept you for who you are, you have to decide whether you can accept your wife for who she is. You can definitely tell your wife how you feel about certain behaviors, but you can't force her to change them, just as she can't force you.

When your wife asks your opinion about something to do with her, remember, sometimes sweet fiction will get you a lot further than a "helpful" direct response.

She's always nagging me about housework.

Let's face it—women do more housework than men, even when they work the same amount of hours outside the

home. So, unless your home is different, your wife is nagging you because you're not doing your share. Chances are, the intensity of your wife's nagging is proportionate to how surprised she is to find herself in this predicament. If you talked a good game about equality before you got married, your wife probably feels angrier than another woman who went into a marriage assuming she would be doing the majority of the housework.

Many men agree in principle that it's only fair that they should share the housework, but in their guts, they don't feel that way at all. So they try flattery and manipulation, something along the order of "I don't know how to sponge mop as well as you do," "You're a better housekeeper than my mother ever was," or "You look really sexy pushing that vacuum cleaner."

If your wife has seen through your ploys, you'll have to change your strategy. If you still hope to avoid housework at all cost, you can suggest that you get a cleaning person. Or you can offer to do other things around the house, like carpentry, grocery shopping, or cooking.

If your wife is determined that you will share the housework, the nagging is not going to go away. In fact, as the years go by it might escalate. Even if your wife doesn't complain much, you can bet she's harboring some resentment about doing the lion's share of the work and she will extract payment for that somewhere else in the relationship. So while you still have a chance at some control, I suggest that you take the bull by the horns; sit down with your wife with a list of *your* preferred chores.

If you continue to avoid your share of the housework and your wife continues to nag, what you have on your hands is a power struggle that is going to permeate every aspect of your relationship. For instance, your wife may

start withholding sex from you, and you might withhold affection from her. Or perhaps she'll form an alliance with the kids against you, and you will stay out late with the guys every time she complains about the chores. Settle the issue by taking responsibility for your share of housekeeping. I know you can probably get away with less, but remember that this is a marriage *partnership*, not a parent-child relationship.

Some wives complain until the cows come home about their husbands' refusal to share the housework but sabotage their husbands' efforts to do so. For instance, if you vacuum the rug as your wife requested and she complains that you didn't do it right, does it over, or asks "Well, did you vacuum?," you're probably not going to vacuum again very soon.

If you decide to pitch in and do your share, tell your wife that you will do it in your fashion and that criticism isn't appreciated. That doesn't mean that when you wash the dishes you leave big globs of food on them. It might mean that the floor isn't waxed to the level of perfection it would be if your wife were doing it.

PMS again?

Although there is speculation that men too have monthly cycles—and there are some wives out there who would be happy to give anecdotal evidence—we all *know* some women have wild mood swings depending on where they are in their monthly cycle. Each woman copes with these hormonal fluctuations in her own way. For instance, some women have no problem saying they are in a bad mood because of PMS, and others deny any suggestion that they're premenstrual.

If your wife is bitchy about everything or sobs uncontrollably over the telephone commercials on TV and you suggest that maybe it's that time of the month, instead of feeling understood, your wife may feel demeaned. The intensity of her feelings seems so fundamental that she may have a hard time "disowning" them by saying "It's just hormones." She may also believe that if *you* think her mood is hormonal, you won't acknowledge her feelings—you'll dismiss them. Her concerns are exacerbated if you have a tendency to attribute normal, run-of-the-mill mood shifts to PMS ("Oh, that time of the month again?"). If you react that way, don't be surprised if she gets angry. Face it—it's not a nice thing to do.

If you're living with a woman who won't acknowledge her PMS for what it is, perhaps you pretend that you don't notice either or secretly keep a little calendar so you know when the bad days are coming. Do you wish she'd just say "I have PMS"? Then tell her. And also tell her that her mood swings are hard on you too. Be matter-of-fact when you say this, not angry.

Perhaps your wife goes in the opposite direction and constantly tells you she has PMS. When you're in the middle of a really good argument, it's annoying and unfair if she suddenly bursts into tears and says "It's not a good time of the month for me."

If you think your wife is using PMS to make excuses for her behavior or to try and get out of doing certain things, call her on it. Say "I'm willing to cut you some slack for PMS, but you're using it as an excuse every time we have a disagreement and you don't like what I have to say."

Everybody has mood changes; some people, more than others. Most husbands and wives learn to work around their spouse's moods. Perhaps rather than experi-

encing PMS your wife is just a moody gal. Your wife's mood fluctuations will be a lot easier to live with if you try to do the following:

- Don't blame yourself for her bad mood.
- Don't take responsibility to change her mood.
- Don't allow her black mood to drag you down.
- Don't get into an argument.

If you show her support yet go on with your life, your wife is free to cope with her moods without facing added problems with you, including having to feel guilty for ruining your day—or life.

Some people manipulate with their moods. If your wife gets angry, withdraws, or slams dishes around to get you to cave in on something, there's only one way to change that behavior: don't cave in. For instance, if you've said you can't get away during the week because you're swamped with work and she's sulking, you can call her on it and tell her you don't like it or ignore it. But don't give in to it. Go on about your business; if she wants to get your attention, she will have to tell you how she feels.

PMS or a bad mood is never an excuse for abusive behavior. If your wife criticizes your daughter ("You're so bossy. No wonder you have no friends") or you ("That was a dumb remark"), tell her it's unacceptable: "You need to find some other way to cope with your feelings than taking them out on your family."

She's always telling me what I can and can't do.

Sometimes men are surprised at the tenacity their wives show about trying to change their behavior. Maybe even

though you show no signs of having changed as a result of her complaints, she still notices in minute detail what you're up to—you ate or drank too much, burped in front of her mother, or made seven insensitive remarks in the course of one hour—and then tells you you should change. Sometimes you feel she's treating you like a kid, not a husband.

Well, do you encourage her? Do you let her buy vitamins for you and remind you to take them, make your yearly doctor appointment, and take the responsibility for cooking healthy meals? Then don't be surprised when she tells you that three doughnuts is not a healthy breakfast, three drinks is enough, or to please not talk with your mouth full.

If you accept and enjoy being mothered by your wife, then you have to take responsibility for your predicament. However, if your wife's mothering is unsolicited and unappreciated, then the next time she mentions the doughnuts, say "I've heard what you have to say about the doughnuts. I don't need any more information."

Men don't try to change their wives nearly as much as women try to change their husbands. This goes back to women's feeling they have to mold those around them. If your wife gets all worked up about your table manners, make an effort to appease her when you go out together. Even if you think it's silly, if your wife is bothered by your clanking your soup spoon against your teeth, try not to do it. However, you can be specific about when and where it's okay for your wife to tell you what's bothering her. For instance, you might tell her that it's absolutely unacceptable for her to say something in front of other people or that you'd rather she left you alone when you're having a perfectly good time and people are enjoying your com-

pany. The point is you are open to listening to your wife's concerns, even willing to adjust your behavior to make her more comfortable, but she has to respect your boundaries.

However, if you feel that your wife is attempting to change you in ways that you don't want to be changed, draw the line. Don't tune out her nagging or agree that you will change a behavior that you have no intention of changing. Be direct. Say "I know you don't like it when I go out with my old frat brothers, but I only see them twice a year. That's not going to change. If it's uncomfortable for you, however, I will understand if you don't want to tag along."

If your wife nags you about something that you've been thinking of changing, don't resist her just because you don't want to do what *she* wants you to. But do ask her to back off. Tell her there is no way you will stop drinking, eating too much, or talking with your mouth full while she complains or nags—it's just human nature. Don't tell her that her nagging makes you want to stuff a Hershey bar in your face right in front of her. Say "The more you bug me, the less likely I am to change."

Once she backs off, give yourself a reasonable amount of time, decide what it is you want to do, and inform your wife of your decision. If you decide to go on a diet, stop drinking or smoking, or start jogging in the mornings, tell her. Also tell her how much, if at all, you want her to be involved.

If you and your wife continue to argue about the same issue without resolution, chances are it's not really about how much you're eating, drinking, or burping but about something else. My guess is you and your wife are focusing on a particular issue and going round and round about it so that you can avoid having a real argument.

Many couples are afraid of out-and-out fighting. You can argue forever without talking about your feelings, but when you fight, you say how you feel and your wife says how she feels, which is often pretty scary. Talking about hurt feelings, disappointments, and anger is difficult. But being able to talk about your feelings is essential to the health of your relationship.

Perhaps you and your wife have had a few fights and avoid them now because they got out of hand with yelling, slamming doors, or saying things you both regret. Having a productive fight is a whole different ballgame: the objective is not to hurt each other but to listen to what the other has to say, have the other listen to you, and come to some *resolution.* A good way to start is to set some ground rules for fighting before you have a fight. For instance, rule out hitting, screaming, name calling, and other forms of abuse. Your wife may request that you don't hold a grudge after the fight, and you might ask that your wife not clam up when she hears something she doesn't like.

Here are a few suggestions to help you get to the real issues:

- Begin your sentences with "I." For instance, say "I feel hurt when you ignore me and talk to the kids" or "I feel angry when you make sarcastic remarks about my eating in front of our friends."
- Stick with the topic. Don't go off on a tangent, and don't let your wife, either. Say "Let's stick to this topic. We can talk about the housework some other time."
- Avoid words like "*always*" or "*never.*"
- Tell her what you want to happen. Make this something your spouse is capable of doing. Otherwise the argu-

ment is not productive. Say "I would like you to stop commenting on my eating habits in front of our friends" or "I want you to pay attention to my feelings as well as to the kids' feelings."

- Don't punish your wife for her feelings. Sometimes what your wife has to say will be hurtful—but true. Listening and being willing to change is what a healthy relationship and personal growth is all about.

I don't want to go to another avant-garde play or to another wedding.

It's a mystery: men make up the majority of composers, conductors, and musicians, yet by and large it's women who drag men to the symphony. I don't get it, but the same goes for museums, art galleries, and those darn avant-garde plays.

Maybe when you were first together, you didn't say no to an avant-garde play, and in turn your then wife-to-be may have gone to a few football games. But as your relationship matures and you feel more confident about each other, it's inevitable that you'll no longer feel the need to share every interest you have. After all, you're not Siamese twins.

If your wife went to concerts and plays with friends before you got married, encourage her to maintain those friendships. Once you tell her you don't mind if she goes out with friends to events you don't particularly enjoy, she may well feel freer to make those plans without you.

If your wife was never comfortable going out alone and is now in heaven because she finally has a partner to

go to all the places she's missed, encourage her to learn to do things alone or to nurture some new friendships. Tell her you're more than happy to go to some events with her but not nearly as many as she would like.

Be a nice guy and go to the events that your wife has a particular interest in and that she really wants to share with you. Have her pick her top ten for the year, and go to those.

If you're disinterested in another out-of-town rodeo, say so, and suggest an alternative. "How about a weekend in Palm Springs instead?"

This brings us to another issue: family functions. I know, sometimes family functions resemble avant-garde plays, but nevertheless, they are your family—or your wife's. Or maybe it's your son's best friend's birthday party. Regardless, many men seem to have an allergy to these sorts of events and often go to great lengths to escape them. Your wife, however, feels it's her *responsibility* to do what's correct, and she will press you to go.

If you're really determined to attend the fewest number of events possible and still hold your marriage, family, and extended family intact, then have your wife tell you what the most important events are and attend those.

In the best of all possible worlds, you would make your best effort to attend affairs. But if you feel strongly that you don't want to attend your mother's second cousin's wedding or go to the opening of a new gallery, then it really is your choice, particularly if you didn't attend these sorts of functions before you were married. Explain your feelings to your wife. Make sure she understands it has nothing to do with her. Also, tell her you take full responsibility for your behavior; in other words, she needn't be

embarrassed or make excuses for you when she gets to the wedding or bar mitzvah. Say "If anyone asks, tell them I don't go to weddings. If they ask why not, tell them to talk to me."

She says I lecture, I say she talks a lot about nothing.

At home most women do more talking than men. When your wife talks with you, she probably wants to engage in some back-and-forth discussion about a particular person, feeling, or aspect of your relationship. Or she may want to just "talk something out," which means she wants you to listen.

Sometimes women do seem to talk about nothing. But your wife feels more connected to you when she's telling you what her friend's cousin said, what the bag lady outside the bank looked like, or how many cars there were on the freeway. You feel no need to chatter about details; in fact, you probably wouldn't even have noticed any of what your wife sees out in the world.

You probably have a tendency to lecture. By this I mean you are likely to pick a topic and expound on it. If your wife mentions something she heard on the news, she certainly wants some discussion about it. But she may be taken aback when you take the opportunity to explain to her exactly how the senate post office works, the historical significance of the Brady bill, or why Democrats deserve the label tax-and-spend liberals.

In response a male friend might debate you on the issue or change the subject. He certainly won't feel insulted or feel he's being lectured to, but your wife probably will. You feel you're just trying to put some meat in the

conversation and that if you don't there's no point in talking.

Neither you nor your wife is right—or wrong. These are basic differences in conversational style, but they can get in the way of having a mutually enjoyable conversation. For instance, you and your wife probably avoid certain topics by now because you know the conversation is likely to break down rapidly into "You're lecturing me" or "This conversation is going nowhere."

What can you do to get over this hump? Well, you can encourage your wife to be more combative in conversations, and you can learn to be more reflective. For instance, if your wife mentions a conflict that occurred at work between her and her boss, instead of talking about employee relations in general, ask her opinion about the conflict. Say "So, what do you think about the disagreement now that it's over?"

Try to choose an appropriate response. For instance, if your wife is feeling bad about a fight she had with her mother, it's probably *not* a good time to tell her your opinion about her family's dynamics. From your point of view, that sort of overview would be helpful, but she'd rather you be supportive and listen to what she's feeling.

When you tell your wife something that happened at work and she offers support, you can tell her that you appreciate her support but you would also like her to play devil's advocate and argue the other side. Tell her you're digging for solutions and if she can challenge your line of reasoning, it will help you to find the best solution.

Both types of communication are useful. Men and women tend to get trapped in one or the other. Your practicing with your wife and her practicing with you enable you both to deploy a variety of conversational skills.

Bibliography

Allman, William F. July 1993. The mating game. *U.S. News and World Report.*

Anderson, Joan Wester. June 8, 1993. Partners in grime. *Woman's Day.*

Baruch, G., and R. Barnett. 1986. Role quality, multiple role involvement, and psychological well-being in midlife women. *Journal of Personality and Social Psychology* 51: 578–585.

Coverman, S. 1989. Women's work is never done: the division of domestic labor. In *Women: A feminist perspective*, ed. Jo Freeman. Mountain View, Ca.: Mayfield.

Eisler, Riane. 1987. *The chalice and the blade: Our history, our future.* Cambridge, Mass.: Harper & Row.

Gibbs, Nancy R. June 28, 1993. Bringing up father. *Time.*

Gray, John. 1993. *Men are from Mars, women are from Venus.* New York: HarperCollins Publishers.

Hochschild, Arlie, and Anne Machung. 1989. *The second shift: working parents and the revolution at home.* New York: Viking.

Klagsbrun, Francine. 1985. *Married people: Staying together in the age of divorce.* New York: Bantam Books.

LaRouche, Janice, and Regina Ryan. 1984. *Janice Larouche's strategies for women at work.* New York: Avon Books.

Lerner, Harriet Goldhor. 1985. *The dance of anger: a woman's guide to changing the patterns of intimate relationships.* New York: Harper & Row.

Meyer, Patricia H. 1980. Between families: The unattached young adult. In *The family life cycle: A framework for family therapy,* ed. Elizabeth A. Carter and Monica McColdrick. New York: Gardner Press, Inc.

Millman, Marcia. 1991. *Warm hearts and cold cash: The intimate dynamics of families and money.* New York: New York Free Press.

Minuchin, Salvador, and H. Charles Fishman. 1981. *Family therapy techniques.* Cambridge, Mass.: Harvard University Press.

Pleck, J. H. 1983. Husband paid work and family roles: Current research issues. In *Jobs and families,* ed. Helena Lopata and Joseph H. Pleck. Current Research on Occupations and Professions Serial, vol. 3. Greenwich: Jai Press.

Reinisch, June M. 1990. *The Kinsey Institute new report on sex.* New York: St. Martin's Press.

Scarf, Maggie. 1987. *Intimate partners: Patterns in love and marriage*. New York: Ballantine Books.

Schor, Juliet. 1991. *The overworked American: The unexpected decline of leisure*. New York: Basic Books.

Tannen, Deborah. 1990. *You just don't understand: Women and men in conversation*. New York: Ballantine Books.

Tavris, Carol. 1989. *Anger: The misunderstood emotion*. New York: Simon & Schuster/Touchstone.